Quality of Experience Paradigm in Multimedia Services

Series Editor
Abdelhamid Mellouk

Quality of Experience Paradigm in Multimedia Services

Application to OTT Video Streaming and VoIP Services

Muhammad-Sajid Mushtaq
Abdelhamid Mellouk

ELSEVIER

First published 2017 in Great Britain and the United States by ISTE Press Ltd and Elsevier Ltd

ISTE Press Ltd
27-37 St George's Road
London SW19 4EU
UK

www.iste.co.uk

Elsevier Ltd
The Boulevard, Langford Lane
Kidlington, Oxford, OX5 1GB
UK

www.elsevier.com

Notices

For information on all our publications visit our website at http://store.elsevier.com/

© ISTE Press Ltd 2017
The rights of Muhammad-Sajid Mushtaq and Abdelhamid Mellouk to be identified as the authors of this work have been asserted by them in accordance with the Copyright, Designs and Patents Act 1988.

British Library Cataloguing-in-Publication Data
A CIP record for this book is available from the British Library
Library of Congress Cataloging in Publication Data
A catalog record for this book is available from the Library of Congress
ISBN 978-1-78548-109-3

Printed and bound in the UK and US

Contents

Introduction

I.1. Motivation

The emerging multimedia services have become the main contributor to the ever increasing Internet Protocol (IP) traffic. Over the last few years, we have been witnessing the tremendous growth of multimedia services, especially online video streaming services, which have prevailed in the global Internet traffic with a larger distinct share. According to a forecast report released by Cisco, the total global consumers of Internet video traffic will be 69% of global consumer Internet traffic in 2017, which is an increase from 57% in 2012. This percentage does not include the video exchange through peer-to-peer (P2P) file sharing. However, if we add all forms of video (TV, video on demand (VoD), Internet and P2P), the sum will be in the range of 80% to 90% of global consumer traffic by 2017 [CIS 13]. Generally, network operators use different methods to improve the end-to-end Quality of Service (QoS); however, these methods are not enough to satisfy the end-user. Therefore, service providers change their strategies from QoS-oriented to user-oriented because high user satisfaction is the main objective of their business.

It is difficult for a network service provider to achieve a high user satisfaction of various network services with different access technologies. Wireless communication systems use different access technologies, ranging from different IEEE standards of wireless local area networks (WLANs) to broadband fourth generation (4G) mobile cellular networks. The Cisco forecast report states that the global mobile data traffic will increase nearly by 11-fold in 2018 [CIS 16]. The multimedia traffic will be the main contributor over the wireless communication system. It is a big challenge for future fifth generation (5G) wireless networks to provide these services in an efficient way in order to deal with end-users' quality expectations. Cloud computing is considered a fundamental part of the next-generation (i.e. 5G) cellular architecture that provides a powerful computing platform to support ultra high-definition video services (e.g. Live IPTV, 2D/3D video, VoD and interactive gaming) to meet the demand of end-users.

Cloud computing improves end-users' experience by managing these services at remote data centers. This trend has led to the emergence of a large number of remote data centers, which is made possible by the availability of fast and reliable Internet networks. With the advent of cloud computing, many applications and services are available to users remotely. As a result, users expect the best network QoS with a high quality standard [JAR 11].

The concept of Quality of Experience (QoE) has recently gained greater attention in both wired and wireless networks, especially in future networks (e.g. 5G). Its main objective is not only to consider and evaluate the network QoS, but also to better estimate the perceived quality of services by customers. In fact, the aim of network service providers is to provide a good user experience with the use of minimum network resources. It is essential for network service providers to consider the impact of each network factor on user perception, because their businesses are highly dependent on users' satisfaction. According to Daniel R. Scoggin, *"The only way to know how customers see your business is to look at it through their eyes"*.

Here are some well-known quotes from industry experts and other people who have highlighted the importance of customer's experience:

"The Customer's perception is your reality".   Kate Zabriskie (Founder, Business Training Works).

"A satisfied customer is the best business strategy of all". Michael LeBoeuf (Businessman).

"The customer experience is the next competitive battleground." Jerry Gregoire (CIO, Dell Computers).

"Your most unhappy customers are your greatest source of learning." Bill Gates (Businessman, Microsoft's Founder).

"Know what your customers want most and what your company does best. Focus on where those two meet." Kevin Stirtz (Book writer, "More Loyal Customers")

"The first step in exceeding your customer's expectation is to know those expectations." Roy H. Williams (Businessman).

In this context, it is necessary to understand the user/customer quality requirements, and hence this objective is defined via the term "QoE". Network service providers and researchers are making strong efforts to develop mechanisms that measure the user-perceived quality while using the multimedia service (e.g. video streaming) [EDU 11]. QoE represents the real quality experience from the users' perspective when they are watching the video streaming or using any other multimedia service. QoE is defined as "the measure of overall acceptability of an application or service perceived subjectively by the end user" [INT 07a]. The European Network on Quality of Experience in Multimedia Systems and Services (Qualinet) [QUA 13] also defines QoE in other perspectives, which are:

"Quality of Experience (QoE) is the degree of delight or annoyance of the user of an application or service. It results from the fulfillment of his or her expectations with respect to the utility and/or enjoyment of the application or service in the light of the user's personality and current state."

QoE: "Degree of delight of the user of a service. In the context of communication services, it is influenced by content, network, device, application, user expectations and goals, and context of use."

The tremendous growth in consumer electronic devices with enhanced capabilities, along with the improved capacities of wireless networks, have led to a vast growth in multimedia services. The new trends in the electronic market have developed a large variety of smart mobile devices (e.g. iPhone, iPad, Android) that are powerful enough to support a wide range of multimedia applications. At the same time, there is an increasing demand for high-speed data services. The 3rd Generation Partnership Project (3GPP) has introduced new radio access technologies, LTE and LTE-Advanced (henceforth referred to as LTE), which can provide large bandwidths and low latencies on a wireless network to fulfill the demand of user equipments (UEs) with acceptable Quality of Service (QoS). A large number of data applications have also been developed for smart mobile devices, which motivate users to access the LTE network more frequently [ETS 11a].

Voice over IP (VoIP) and video streaming are key multimedia traffic services that are widely used. VoIP is a popular low-cost service for voice calls over IP networks. The success of VoIP is mainly influenced by user satisfaction with respect to quality of calls when compared with conventional fixed telephone services. The main challenge for VoIP service is to provide the same QoS as that of a conventional telephone network, i.e. reliable and with a QoS guarantee. In conventional networks, the bearer quality is managed as a single quality plan, while in next-generation networks (NGNs), it is necessary to manage the end-user's QoE. In a wireless system, the unpredictable air interface behaves differently for each UE. In these circumstances, it is necessary to monitor the QoE in the network on a call-by-call basis [ETS 02]. We consider the VoIP traffic in the LTE scheduler to allocate the radio resource based on the user's QoE.

Video streaming is a main and growing contributor to Internet traffic. This growth results from deep changes in the technologies that are used for delivering video content to end-users over the Internet. To meet the high expectation of users, it is necessary to analyze video streaming services thoroughly in order to find out the degree of influence of technical and non-technical parameters on user satisfaction. Among these factors, we can find network parameters, which represent the QoS. Delay, jitter and packet loss are the main parameters of QoS, which have a strong influence on user (dis)satisfaction. In addition to network parameters, other external environmental factors, such as video parameters, terminal types and psychological factors, have a great impact on user-perceived quality.

In general, researchers use two methods to assess the quality of multimedia services: the subjective method and the objective method. The subjective method was proposed by the International Telecommunication Union Telecommunication Standardization Sector (ITU-T), which is used to find out the user perception of the quality of video streaming. The mean opinion score (MOS) is an example of the subjective measurement method, in which users rate the video quality by giving five different scores from 5 (best quality) to 1 (worst quality). In contrast, the objective method uses different models of human expectations and tries to estimate the performance of a video service in an automated manner, without human intervention. The subjective and objective methods have their own importance in evaluating the QoE, and they complement each other instead of replacing each other. It is very difficult to measure the MOS of in-service speech quality subjectively, because MOS is a numerical average value of a large number of user opinions. Therefore, many objective speech quality measurement methods have been developed to make a good estimation of MOS. The E-model [INT 11] and perception evaluation of speech quality (PESQ) [INT 01a] are objective methods for measuring MOS scores. The PESQ cannot be used to monitor the QoE for real-time calls, because it uses a reference signal and compares it with the real-degraded signal to calculate the MOS score. Therefore, we have used the E-model computational method to calculate the MOS score of conversation quality by using the latency (delay), and the packet loss rate by using the transmission rating factor (R-factor) [INT 11].

I.2. Research projects

Many research projects have highlighted the importance and role of QoE to reshape the multimedia applications and content distribution systems, some of which are given below:

1) Quality of experience for augmented telepresence (QoEAT)

Consortium members: Mid Sweden University, Acreo, Akilt Communications AB and HIAB

Period: 01-01-2017 to 12-31-2018.

The objective of QoEAT research project is to investigate the QoE for augmented telepresence. In the QoEAT, the user's QoE is very important because users will perform the complex tasks remotely, which highly demands a strong and clear vision. Telepresence is considered as a high video conferencing where user-perceived quality experience is good enough for remote participation, as they are physically present. However, augmented reality refers to the inclusion of artificial information from the database or image analysis in real time. This project defines the augmented telepresence as a combination of high-quality video conferencing and information from the database, data or image analysis in real time to operate a vehicle (e.g. crane) from the remote location.

2) Monitoring and control of QoE in large-scale media distribution architectures (MONALIS)

Consortium members: Indra Sistemas, Orange Polska S.A., Mint Media sp. z o.o., National Institute of Telecommunications, Instituto de Telecomunicações, Alcatel-Lucent España SA, Networker QoS Oy, VTT Technical Research Centre of Finland Ltd, Accanto Systems Oy, Netplaza Oy, Creanord Ltd, Elisa Corporation and Starhome

Period: 10-01-2016 to 12-31-2018.

The MONALIS project focuses on monitoring and control of QoE in large-scale media distribution architectures. This project will develop monitoring tools for analyzing the Big Data to evaluate user satisfaction in terms of QoE. The measurement platforms will measure the data from low-level packet information in the network to the upper-level user's QoE. The different actors in the multimedia delivery chain will monitor and exchange the QoE-relevant data. A new business model will be developed that takes the advantage of a Big Data framework to optimize their resources and increase the revenue.

3) Next-generation over-the-top multimedia services (NOTTS)

Consortium members: Indra Sistemas, Alcatel Lucent, Dycec, ADTEL Sistemas de Telecomunicacion, Acreo, Ericsson AB, Alkit Communication, Procera Networks, Lund University, Institut Telecom SudParis, University Paris-Est Créteil, IP-Label, Thomson Video Networks, VTT Technical Research Centre of Finland, Anvia Oyj, Hibox Systems Oy Ab, Networker QoS Oy, Oy Omnitele Ab, Orange Polska S.A. and Portugal Telecom Inovação e Sistemas

Period: 05-01-2013 to 03-31-2016.

The NOTTS project addresses the deficiency of the current Internet architecture and business model, which are not developed to cater for the massive deployment of OTT services. The project has developed a complete media distribution area, which has a huge potential and increasing annual turnover. The goal of the project is to provide an integrated solution for European OTT service providers that contains all the comprehensive methods and techniques to develop a context and media-aware delivery platform.

4) Quality of experience estimators in networks (QuEEN)

Consortium members: Acreo AB, BTH - Blekinge Institute of Technology, Embou, Ericsson AB, EXFO Nethawk, France Telecom, FTW - Telecommunications Research Center Vienna, Hiberus TECNOLOGÍA, IBBT, INDRA sistemas, Info24, Institut National de Recherche en Informatique et en Automatique (INRIA), Instituto Tecnológico de Aragón, IP-Label Newtest, Mobisoft Oy, PPO Yhtiöt Oy, Rugged Tooling Oy, Technical University Berlin, Telnet Redes Inteligentes, University of Zagreb - Faculty of EE and Computing and VTT Technical Research Center of Finland

Period: 01-09-2011 to 31-08-2014.

The aim of the QuEEN project is to develop an overlay network software agent for estimating the multiservice QoE to represent a human user. The user agent communicates with other user agents by sharing the profile information about the network so that services and applications can adapt to both-end preferences and expectations on a peer-to-peer basis. Similarly, the service provider obtains relevant QoE information and optimizes its network resources to achieve the desired user satisfaction and reduce the operational cost (e.g. cloud paradigm).

5) IP network monitoring for quality of service intelligent support (IPNQSIS)

Consortium members: Indra Sistemas, Alcatel Lucent, Dycec, Gigle Semiconductors, Naudit SL, Soft Telecom, Acreo AB, Alkit Communications AB, Ericsson AB, Lund University, Procera Networks, Institut Telecom SudParis, IP-Label Newtest, Vierling Communication SAS, Université Paris-Est Créteil, EXFO NetHawk, PPO-Yhtiöt Oy and VTT Technical Research Centre

Period: 10-01-2010 to 04-30-2013.

The main objective of the IPNQSIS project is to develop a customer experience management (CEM) architecture. The project is based on the study of QoE, which analyzes the performance of networks and services and observes their impact on end-users. Based on this study, IPNQSIS develops a continuous monitoring system to build a complete customer experience management system (CEMS). Deep packet/flow inspection methods are used to monitor and analyze the IP traffic, leading to new multimedia content distribution methods and solutions to maintain acceptable user's QoE.

I.3. Book structure

This book is organized as follows:

Chapter 1 reviews the general literature and related works done in relation to this research work. The chapter is divided into three sections that correspond to the contribution of each chapter. The analysis of QoE is not an easy task because all the factors that directly or indirectly influence the user-perceived quality have to be considered. Researchers use distinct methods to correlate the network QoS parameters with user's QoE. The developed methods are mostly based on testbed experiments that involve different equipments, methods and tools. Datasets are collected at the end of a testbed experiment and are analyzed to observe the influence of different factors on user's QoE. The user's profile is also built up based on testbed experiments. In addition, a comprehensive detail is given on the video streaming technologies for HTTP-based unmanaged networks and important adaptive video streaming technologies that have been developed by well-known companies such as Adobe, Microsoft, Apple and 3GPP/MPEG. The chapter briefly describes video streaming technologies, important video delivery components and a general overview of famous adaptive streaming methods. Rate-adaptive video streaming approaches are evaluated using the testbed experiment, considering the performance parameters of three important elements (client, server and network) to evaluate the proposed methods. Then, the chapter focuses on LTE-A networks and discusses various scheduling methods that are used to allocate radio resources to the UE based on different criteria by taking into account different parameters. The chapter also discusses the role of the power-saving method in the context of different wireless systems, and highlights its impact on the system's performance. Finally, the chapter describes two main aspects of 5G networks: (i) QoE using multimedia services (VoIP and video) and (ii) power-saving model for mobile device using DRX states of the UE and virtual base station (VBS) using the component-based strategy.

Chapter 2 discusses two approaches to collecting a subjective dataset for assessing the user's QoE while using video services. These approaches consist of a controlled and an uncontrolled environmental framework. In the controlled environment, a laboratory testbed is carried out to collect datasets and the user's QoE with respect to different parameters (QoS parameters, video characteristic, device type, etc.). The data is stored in the form of a MOS value. This data is then used to analyze the correlation between QoS and QoE by using the six machine learning (ML) classifiers. The data also consists of users' profile built up by collecting the information from users. This profile is used to investigate the impact of different parameters on user perception. In the uncontrolled environment, an application tool based on crowdsourcing is described, which can be used to investigate users' QoE in a real environment. It subjectively collects users' opinion about video quality, and during the watching of the video, it stores the parameters' real-time network performance in a local SQL database. In addition, the tool measures and stores the real-time performance characteristics of the end-user device in terms of system memory, performance capacity, CPU usage and other parameters.

Chapter 3 describes the general video rate-adaptive system and highlights the important role of key elements in regulating video streaming services at the client side. It discusses the adaptive video streaming architecture that mainly consists of three components: client, delivery network and server. The chapter proposes a new client-based rate-adaptive video streaming algorithm that dynamically selects the suitable video segment based on dynamic network conditions, and client parameters. The proposed BBF method takes into account three important QoS parameters in order to regulate the user's QoE for video streaming services over HTTP, which are: bandwidth, buffer and dropped frame rate (BBF). The BBF is evaluated with different buffer lengths, and the results indicate that a greater buffer length is less affected by dynamic bandwidth, but it does not efficiently utilize network resources. The performance of the BBF method is compared with Adobe's OSMF streaming method, and the results show that the BBF method effectively manages a sudden decrease in bandwidth and dropped frame rate when the client system does not have enough resources to decode the frames. In the case of a lower buffer length, the BBF switches to the lower video quality and optimizes the user's QoE by avoiding stalling and pausing during the video playback.

Chapter 4 presents the general overview of the LTE-A wireless network. It focuses on the downlink scheduling method because downlink is more important than uplink because of high-traffic flows. The QoE-based LTE-A downlink scheduling algorithm is proposed for delay-sensitive multimedia traffic (VoIP). The general architecture of a LTE-A scheduler, the elements that play an important role in scheduling and three communication layers of the LTE-A network are presented. The performance of the proposed downlink scheduler, i.e. QoE power efficient method (QEPEM), is evaluated along with efficient power utilization of the UE. The goal is to develop a downlink scheduling algorithm that allocates radio resources to the UE by taking into account the user's QoE along with the power-saving method, i.e. discontinuous reception (DRX). The performance of the QEPEM is evaluated and compared with traditional scheduling methods such as proportional fair (PF) and best channel quality indicator (BCQI). The QEPEM tries to enhance the QoE and provides better QoS by decreasing packet losses, improving fairness among UEs and considering the QoS requirement of multimedia service (e.g. delay). Simulation results show that the QEPEM performs better than traditional schedulers with better user experience, because it allocates resources efficiently among UEs.

Chapter 5 focuses on two main aspects of 5G networks: (i) QoE using multimedia services (VoIP and video) and (ii) power-saving model for mobile device and virtual base station (VBS). First, it describes an analytical method that minimizes the overall network delay for multimedia services including constant bitrate (VoIP) and variable bitrate (video) traffic models. In addition, it proposes a new method that measures the user's QoE for video streaming traffic using network QoS parameters, i.e. delay and packet loss rate. The performance of the proposed QoE method is compared with the Quality of Video (QoV) method. The results indicate that the QoE method performs best by carefully handling the impact of QoS parameters, i.e. it successfully reduces the overall network delays, thereby maximizing the user's QoE. Second, it discusses a method that calculates the power consumption of a 5G network by considering its main elements based on the current vision of the 5G network infrastructure. The proposed model uses the component-based methodology that simplifies the process by taking into account various high power-consuming elements. The method is evaluated by considering three UE's DRX models and VBS with respect to different DRX timers and performance parameters such as power-saving (PS) and delay.

The last chapter concludes the book and includes future investigations. It summarizes the results of the different methods that we used to investigate the concept of QoE for multimedia services through the analysis of technical and non-technical parameters. It also addresses the challenges of investigating users' QoE for multimedia services and highlights the impacts of different parameters on user perception. Finally, it proposes several future directions to further explore the influence of different factors on user's QoE.

1

Background and Contextual Study

In this chapter, we review the literature with respect to the related work. We divide the related work into three main sections that represent the contribution of each work presented in the following chapters. First, we present different methods that are generally used to collect the Quality of Experience (QoE) dataset. This dataset is used to investigate the impact of different parameters on the user-perceived QoE. It also contains the user's profile that has the user's personal details and other key information related to the service under testing. Second, we review different standards and rate-adaptive video streaming methods proposed in the literature. Third, we discuss various scheduling methods that allocate resources to user equipments (UEs) by considering different Quality of Service (QoS) parameters and other elements including power status.

1.1. Introduction

The multimedia video service started in the middle of the last century and spread out rapidly with the introduction of television. In the late 1990's, Internet service enabled the viewing of online recorded videos. Later, with the continuous innovation in Internet broadband service, network service providers offered more capacity and high-speed download links to end-users, which made the video streaming service boom over the Internet protocol (IP) network. Cisco predicts that the total number of global consumers of Internet video traffic will be 69% of all the consumer Internet traffic in 2017 [CIS 13]. Nowadays, we can watch online video content easily, thanks to the availability of a large variety of consumer electronic devices. The remarkable growth in video-enabled electronic devices, such as personal computers (PCs), smartphones, tablets and Internet-enabled television, and the accessibility of high-speed Internet (WiFi/3G/4G) are key factors for the growing popularity of online video contents. The earlier trends of TV have changed quickly. It has now reached a point where it meets consumers' expectation by making video services available on any device over any network connection and also delivering the same high-quality service found in a conventional TV.

With the big advancement in the core and radio link capacity, the future 5th Generation (5G) networks have been expected to provide high-speed links (up to 10 Gbps) to each user [HUA 14a]. The enhancement of the wireless communication system opens a new door of opportunity for always providing a high definition (HD) video streaming to users. The world trend is moving towards "Everything over IP", and the important benefit of future 5G networks is to provide different types of services, e.g. voice, text and high-quality video, by using the IP network. The IP infrastructure is quickly replacing the traditional system to offer more services to users at low cost. IP networks offer best-effort services; therefore, packet loss, delay, jitter and throughput can degrade the QoS of video streaming, which in turn degrades the QoE. The Internet is an unmanaged network, and transmission of video streaming requires new mechanisms to provide high-quality video streaming to users, as expected from managed TV delivery networks.

1.2. Subjective test

The Internet is a collection of diverse networks, where video delivery from source to destination is carried out through distinct unique elements with complex interactions. Video service is more susceptible to impairment and problems than data and voice services. In a video service, the user has no second chance for retransmission of lost data because the impact of lost video packets can be observed, while in a data service, the user is unaware about the retransmission of lost data. The network QoS is a key factor that influences the user-perceived QoE. Many studies have been conducted to correlate QoS with QoE for capturing the degree of user entertainment. Other techniques have also been developed to evaluate and predict users' QoE, in order to deliver a better quality of service to end-users. In the controlled environment, many testbed studies involving different tools, equipment and methods have been conducted.

1.2.1. *Controlled environment approach*

The controlled environment approach refers to the laboratory testbed experiment, in which all environmental factors are fixed and influence the user-perceived QoE. The International Telecommunication Union Telecommunication Standardization Sector (ITU-T) has defined the recommendation criteria to set up and carry out the laboratory testbed experiment [INT 08]. In [MOK 11], a testbed experiment was proposed to explore how the network QoS affects the QoE of HTTP video streaming. In [FRE 11], a testbed was carried out to collect data using 10 participants, correlating stream state data with video quality ratings. These datasets were used to develop self-healing networks, i.e. networks possessing the ability to detect the degradation of video streaming QoE, and react and troubleshoot network issues. The correlation of QoE with QoS was studied in [TRU 12] by controlling QoS network parameters (e.g. packet loss, jitter, delay). Because subjective campaigns are by nature limited in size and number of participants, it is impossible to cover all the possible configurations and parameter values. However, a QoE prediction model was proposed in [AGB 08] for unseen cases based primarily on limited subjective tests. This model reduces the need for cumbersome subjective tests but at the price of reduced accuracy. To overcome the weakness of [AGB 08], a learning-based prediction model was proposed in [MEN 09]. In [MEN 10], a machine learning technique was proposed using a subjective quality feedback. This technique is used to model the dependencies of different QoS parameters related to the network and application layer on the QoE of network services, thereby considered as an accurate QoE prediction model.

Extensive research work has been carried out to provide application services with acceptable quality. Researchers have studied different techniques to correlate the network's QoS with user-perceived QoE. Other methods have also been developed to provide better QoS for evaluating and predicting the user's QoE. Generally, the developed methods are studied and examined in the form of experiments by setting up the testbed that consists of different equipment, methods and tools. Datasets collected at the end of the testbed experiment are analyzed by observing the impact of different factors subjectively perceived by end-users. The user's profile is also built up as an outcome of this testbed.

In [KIM 12], a testbed experiment was carried out to assess the QoE model for video streaming services using QoS parameters in the wired/wireless network. In that study, the authors considered only QoS parameters to estimate the user-perceived QoE and not the important information related to users' profiles. Similarly, a testbed experiment was carried out by [MOK 11] who also considered only QoS parameters and investigated how QoS networks affected the QoE of HTTP video streaming. In [KIM 08], the authors proposed an objective method for measuring the QoE by using QoS parameters. In that study, they proposed a QoS and QoE correlation model and the QoE evaluation method using QoS parameters in the converged network environment. Many research works have been carried out to predict the QoE based on QoS parameters. The correlation between QoE and QoS was studied in [TRU 12], where the authors investigated how the controlled QoS network parameters (e.g. packet loss, jitter, delay) influenced the QoE. In [HOS 11a], the authors highlighted the problem with the existing QoE model, which does not take into account the past experience of user satisfaction when using a certain service. This important psychological influence factor is called the memory effect, which plays a vital role in meeting end-users' expectation for a better QoE. Many studies have been carried out on users' profiles, but most of them are related to the World Wide Web (WWW). Therefore, it is important for the service provider to find out the pattern that clearly points out the use of information at the end system. In [CHE 09], the authors used the fuzzy clustering algorithm to analyze the user's e-learning behavior. The cluster analysis helps the teacher to understand students in a better way by considering their interest, personality and other information. In [TEE 05], the authors described a method that presents the information to the end-user by considering the user's profile. The user's profile is a key factor that can be helpful for network service providers to offer a service acceptable for end-users. In our work, we investigate the statistical analysis of QoS parameters and their impact on end-users. This will help network service providers to utilize their resources efficiently and get high user satisfaction by maintaining a certain threshold of QoS parameters.

1.2.2. *Uncontrolled environment approach*

Investigating QoE is not a simple task because all the variables that directly or indirectly influence the user-perceived quality should be considered. Researchers have studied different techniques to correlate the QoS network with end-user's QoE. Other methods have also been developed to provide a better QoS in order to evaluate and predict the end-user's QoE. It is generally considered that providing a better network QoS will result in good QoE, which is true to some extent. However, always providing good parameters of QoS network will not guarantee end-user satisfaction due to some uncontrollable or external environmental factors such as video parameters, terminal characteristics and psychological factors.

In the uncontrolled environment, the crowdsourcing method is an alternative to the laboratory testing approach for assessing the QoE of video services. In the crowdsourcing environment, a testing task (e.g. video) is allocated to a large group of anonymous users who can participate in the testing task from different parts of the world via the Internet using their own devices. In [KIM 12], a testbed experiment was carried out to assess the QoE model for video streaming services using QoS parameters in the wired/wireless network. In that study, the authors considered only QoS parameters to estimate the user-perceived QoE and not the important information related to the user's profile and terminal properties. In [MOK 11], QoE was evaluated for HTTP video streaming. In that study, the authors used different QoS network parameters (e.g. packet loss, delay and throughput) and observed the impact of QoS parameters in the form of stalling event. The testbed was carried out in a controlled environment (laboratory), and each test condition used only one video streaming clip with a total of 10 users. In that study, the authors did not consider the terminal properties, and the lower number of participants providing their QoE based on one video did not reflect the reliability of QoE. In [HOS 11b], a crowdsourcing approach was presented to assess the QoE of a TCP-based online video streaming service, YouTube. In that study, the authors considered only the influence of the stalling event (as a key factor) on user-perceived quality. They did not take into account the QoS parameters and terminal characteristics that have a greater impact on QoE.

To assess the QoE, a Web-based crowdsourcing platform was presented in [CHE 10]. This platform was designed to provide administrative control to researchers, which defines the type of multimedia test and registers or updates experiment profiles, setting or description of the crowdsourcing test, and after the test, the results log files can be downloaded. The participant of the test also gets a reward as a payment. The reliability of the end results cannot be proved due to the following reasons: when participants are remote and unknown; when participants may submit incorrect results to earn more money by completing more tests; when participants cannot understand the test description correctly and complete the task incorrectly. In [HOS 11b] and [GAR 12], the authors used the paid crowdsourcing platform called microworkers. Microworkers has numerous registered workers who participate in crowdsourcing experiments. This is also a paid platform that can have the same problems as discussed earlier. In this work, we present our developed crowdsourcing framework to assess the QoE of online video streaming. It is a user-friendly framework, which is easy to install and can be used without any complexity. The proposed framework has the ability to capture and store important information that helps in analyzing and evaluating the QoE.

1.3. HTTP-based video streaming technologies

Video streaming services run over either a managed network or an unmanaged network. In a managed network, video services use multicast transport and maintain the required QoS characteristics, such as cable and IPTV services. By contrast, when video services are run over an unmanaged network, achieving certain QoS characteristics becomes a challenging task. The main video streaming technologies that run over unmanaged networks are Adobe Flash, Apple QuickTime, Microsoft Windows Media. In addition, the emerging adaptive video streaming technologies are Adobe's HTTP Dynamic Streaming (HDS), Apple's HTTP Live Streaming (HLS), Microsoft Smooth Streaming (MSS) and MPEG's Dynamic Adaptive Streaming over HTTP (DASH). These streaming technologies send the video content to the end user using the unicast connection. Here, we will briefly discuss the video streaming technologies that run over unmanaged networks.

The media streaming content is transmitted among different end users over IP networks by using distinct methods. Generally, an appropriate method is selected based on the type of media content and underlying network conditions, because it requires a certain level of QoS characteristics such as low packet loss, jitter, delay and efficient transmission. The media streaming protocol defines the structure of packets and the transmission method. Nowadays, many protocols are implemented for efficient media streaming, which can be classified into two categories: push-based and pull-based protocols [BEG 11].

– Push-based media streaming protocols

In push-based media streaming protocols, when the server and the client connection is established, the server will push the media content (packets) to the client until the client ends the session. It is a server-driven approach where a server maintains the session and listens to messages from the client to change the session state. The well-known session control protocol used in push-based media streaming is the Real-Time Streaming Protocol (RTSP). Push-based protocols generally use the Real-Time Transport Protocol (RTP) along with User Datagram Protocol (UDP). In the RTP/UDP, the client/server communication relies on application-level implementation when compared with the underlying transport protocol [BEG 11], where the RTP performs best for low delay and best-effort transmission. In the conventional push-based method, the server encodes the media content according to the client's consumption capacity and maintains a certain buffer level to avoid buffer underflow by switching to a lower bitrate stream.

– Pull-based media streaming protocols

In pull-based media streaming protocols, the client plays a key role in making a decision requesting for the appropriate content from the media server. Therefore, the server is active only to respond to the client's requests, otherwise it is in an idle state. The client requests the media streaming content based on device properties and network bandwidths. HTTP is the main protocol for Internet download, which is also the principal protocol for pull-based media delivery. The progressive download method is an example of the pull-based protocol, which is widely used for downloading media streaming over IP networks. In pull-based streaming protocols, the client avoids the buffer underflow by using the bitrate adaptation method, where a client requests the suitable media segment based on device states and available network bandwidths.

1.3.1. *Video streaming method*

HTTP video streaming is highly dominant due to the availability of Internet support on many devices, which, unlike other media transport protocols such as RTP/RTSP, easily traverses NATs and firewalls. Both the progressive download and adaptive streaming methods use HTTP as a primary protocol to transport the media content to the client. HTTP-based servers are more scalable than push-based streaming servers, because they maintain minimum state information at the server side. HTTP video streaming is easier and cheaper to move data closer to network users, and the video file segment is like a normal web object. It also provides an opportunity to content delivery networks to increase their scalability of content distribution [BEG 11].

1.3.1.1. *Progressive download*

Initially, HTTP-based video streaming applications used the progressive download method (HTTP over TCP), and thanks to its simplicity, this method has become very popular for viewing online video contents. In the progressive download method, the client requests the download of a video content from the server using an HTTP-based command that quickly begins to pull the content from the server before the whole video is downloaded. The client player starts playing the video, when a desired minimum buffer level is full-up, and it continues playback of the video without any interruption, until a suffcient client buffer level is filled. Buffer underflow can occur when the playback rate is more than the download rate due to an insufficient network bandwidth.

This method has some limitation which degrades the QoE, because it lacks the rich features of video streaming, e.g. trick modes such as fast forward seek/play and rewind, and suffers from constant freezing or rebuffering due to the shortage of bandwidth. The new emerging approach to adaptive streaming not only replaces the progressive download, but also overcomes the shortcoming issues. Adaptive streaming is a pull-based media streaming approach that consists of the progressive download and a streaming method [BEG 11].

1.3.1.2. *Adaptive streaming*

The innovation in HTTP video streaming was started by Move Networks, which is called adaptive streaming. Adaptive streaming increases the quality and resolution of video content according to the handling ability of the user device throughout the data network. The adaptive streaming server maintains different copies of the same video content that vary in bitrate, and clients can switch to a high-quality content according to the available bandwidth. Although a number of adaptive video streaming methods, such as 3GPP's Adaptation HTTP Streaming (AHS) release 9 specification and HTTP Adaptive Streaming (HAS) in Open TV Forum, are available but they have not fully penetrated the market.

1.3.2. *Adaptive video delivery components*

Adaptive video streaming has some new functionalities that must be added in networks, and service providers must implement fundamental content delivery network components. The most important components in HTTP adaptive video streaming are transcoder/encoder, packager (also called fragmenter, segmenter and chunking) and content delivery network, as shown in Figure 1.1.

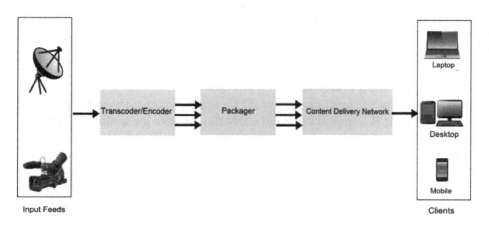

Figure 1.1. *Adaptive video delivery components*

1.3.2.1. *Transcoder/encoder*

The main function of the transcoder/encoder is to prepare the media file for the packager. It takes the incoming baseband or IP digital video and converts it into a multi-stream output profile of different bitrates and resolutions that are suitable for the end-user device. The transcoder/encoder provides different profiles for each input video, because an end-user's QoE mainly depends on the number of profiles. A large number of profiles results in supporting more devices and a better QoE, but it requires more space on the server.

1.3.2.2. Packager

Adaptive streaming uses the stateless protocol (HTTP), where the video file is broken into small pieces of HTTP files, i.e. fragments, segments or chunks. The process of fragmentation, segmentation or chunking can be done in the transcoder, or it can be processed to the packager component. Each segment generally lasts between 2 and 10 seconds. It supports live streaming as well as on-demand video. The packager is the central main component of the adaptive streaming system, which takes the output from the transcoder and converts the video for delivery according to the protocol. The video segment is delivered either through the HTTP pull or HTTP PUT/POST command. The packager has encryption capability: it encrypts each outgoing segment in the compatible format for the delivery protocol. It also works with a third-party key management system that manages and distributes the key to end-users. The generation of the manifest or playlist is a key function of this component.

1.3.2.3. Content delivery network

A content delivery network (CDN) is based on generic HTTP server/caches for streaming the video contents over HTTP, which requires specialized servers at each node. It is important that the CDN should have the ability to handle a large number of segments as well as support a substantial amount of video content.

1.4. HTTP-based adaptive video streaming methods

HTTP-based adaptive video streaming has become an attractive method for service providers. It not only uses the existing infrastructure of web downloading (thus saving an extra cost), but also changes the quality of the video (bitrate) according to the available bandwidth to increase the user-perceived quality. Initially, it was considered that the Transmission Control Protocol (TCP) was not suitable for video streaming due to its properties such as reliability and congestion control. Indeed, a reliable data transmission can cause a large retransmission delay, and congestion control can cause a throughput variation. Consequently, earlier researchers considered the UDP as the underlying transport protocol, as it is an unreliable connectionless protocol that simplifies data transmission. Later on, it was proved that TCP mechanisms for reliable data transmission and congestion control do not effectively degrade video quality, especially if the client player can adapt to the large throughput variation. Additionally, the use of the TCP over HTTP does not lead to the problem of data filtering (through firewalls and NATs), because they allow the HTTP file to pass through port 80, like regular web objects.

Initially, HTTP-based video streaming application used the progressive download method (HTTP over TCP), and thanks to its simplicity, this method became very popular for viewing online video contents. However, this method has some limitations in that it degrades the QoE, because it lacks the rich features of video streaming, e.g. trick modes such as fast forward seek/play and rewind, and suffers from constant freezing or rebuffering due to the shortage of bandwidth. The new emerging approach to adaptive streaming not only replaces the progressive download, but also overcomes these shortcoming issues. Adaptive streaming is a pull-based media streaming approach that consists of the progressive download and a streaming method [BEG 11].

The evolution of adaptive video streaming has led to a new set of standards from well-known organizations, such as Adobe, Microsoft, Apple and 3GPP/MPEG. These standards are widely adopted because they increase the user's QoE by providing video services over HTTP, but in an adaptive manner, according to network conditions and device characteristics. The HTTP adaptive streaming technologies provided by these organizations are Adobe's HDS, MSS, Apple's HLS, and MPEG's DASH.

1.4.1. *Traditional streaming versus adaptive streaming*

In traditional IP streaming, the video is delivered to users through a number of proprietary "stateful" protocols such as RTSP (Real-Time Streaming Protocol), Adobe's RTMP (Real-Time Messaging Protocol), and Microsoft's MMS (Microsoft Media Server). These protocols make a dynamic point-to-point link between user devices and the streaming server to handle the state of the video. The user and the server must have synchronized video states, e.g. play, pause, stop, etc. Traditional video streaming is generally delivered over UDP, an unreliable connectionless protocol that degrades the user's QoE because of packet losses. The complex synchronization between the client and the server allows traditional video streaming to adapt the variation in network bandwidth, but as an outcome, those adaptive protocols are not widely adopted due to their complexity. The RTSP is a good example of a traditional video streaming protocol, as shown in Figure 1.2, where the client connects to the video streaming server until it sends a disconnection request to the server, and the server keeps monitoring the state of the client. The default packet size of the RTSP is 1452 bytes. When a video is encoded at the rate of 1 Mbps, each packet will carry approximately 11 milliseconds of video.

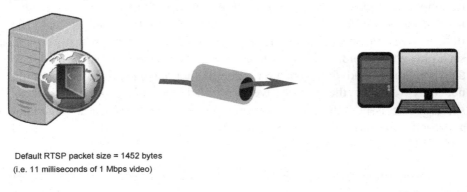

Default RTSP packet size = 1452 bytes
(i.e. 11 milliseconds of 1 Mbps video)

Video Server   Client

Figure 1.2. *RTSP Traditional Video Streaming*

Similarly, the success of HTTP technologies provides the opportunity to develop CDNs, and network operators can effectively manage the "stateless" HTTP protocol networks. The innovation in HTTP video streaming was started by Move Networks, which is called adaptive streaming. This adaptive streaming increases the quality and resolution of video contents according to the handling ability of the user device throughout the data network. The adaptive streaming server maintains different copies of the same video content that vary in bitrate, and the client can switch to a high-quality content according to the available bandwidth.

In HTTP adaptive streaming, the source video content (either a file or live stream) is broken into file segments, called fragments, chunks or segments, using the desired format, which contain video codec, audio codec, encryption protocol, etc. Each segment is generally between 2 and 10 seconds of the stream. The segment file consists of either a multiplexing container that mixes the data from different tracks (video, audio, subtitles, etc.) or a single track. The stream is divided into chunks at the boundaries of a video group of pictures (GOP), identified by an IDR frame. IDR is a frame that can be decoded independently, without looking for other frames, and each chunk does not depend on previous and successive chunks. The file segments are hosted on a regular HTTP server. The general HTTP adaptive streaming is shown in Figure 1.3.

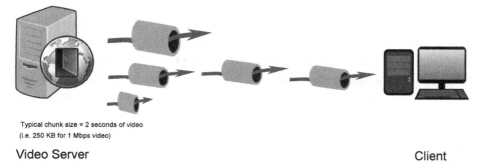

Typical chunk size = 2 seconds of video
(i.e. 250 KB for 1 Mbps video)

Video Server   Client

Figure 1.3. *Adaptive Video Streaming*

Video adaptive methods can be divided into three main categories: 1) transcoding-based, 2) scalable encoding-based and 3) multiple bitrate switching.

1) Transcoding-based: this adapts the video content that corresponds to a specific bitrate during on-the-fly transcoding of the raw data [PRA 08]. This technique is good because it can limit the frame rate, compression and video resolution. However, it requires more processing power and has poor scalability, because transcoding is done separately for each client, and thus it is difficult to implement in CDNs.

2) Scalable encoding-based: an important adaptation method that uses scalable codecs such as H264/MPEG-4 SVC [KRA 03, KUS 10]. Without

recoding the raw video data, both spatial and temporal scalability are successfully achieved to adapt the video resolution and frame rate. This method has the advantage over the transcoding-based technique, because it reduces the processing load by encoding the raw video date one time and uses the scalability features of the encoder to adapt on the fly. However, this approach has limitations, e.g. it cannot be used in CDNs because a special server is required for adaptation logic, while the content cannot be cached in standard proxies. Additionally, the video adaptation decision-making depends on the codec used that restricts the video content provider to using limited codecs [DEC 14b].

3) Multiple bitrate or stream switching: it is a streaming method adopted by leading streaming systems such as Adobe's HDS, MSS [BOC 13], Apple's HLS, Netflix (popular for its video-on-demand service) [NET 15a] and Move Networks (popular for live services of several TV networks) [NET 15b]. MPEG introduced the DASH method to promote the standardization and compatibility of stream switching systems [SOD 11]. It is standardized by ISO to transport the adaptive streaming over HTTP using the existing infrastructure [ISO 13]. The raw video content is encoded into different bitrates that results in many versions of a single video, and the streaming method selects the suitable video bitrate version according to the user's available bandwidth. This method has the advantage of reducing the processing load because one-time video encoding is required, and later no more processing is needed to adapt the video according to the variable bandwidth. It also does not depend on employed codec, and the encoder can work efficiently for each video quality level or version. The main disadvantage is that more storage space is required, and the adaptation process only selects the available discrete video quality. The description of four popular adaptive video streaming methods is briefly provided to summarize their functionality.

The evolution of adaptive video streaming has led to a new set of standards from well-known organizations, such as Adobe, Microsoft, Apple and MPEG. These standards are widely adopted as they increase the user's QoE by streaming the video service over HTTP, but in an adaptive manner, according to network conditions and device characteristics. The HTTP adaptive streaming technologies provided by these organizations are Adobe's HDS, MSS, Apple's HLS and 3GPP/MPEG's DASH.

1.4.2. *Adobe's HTTP Dynamic Streaming (HDS)*

Adobe's HDS uses the MP4 fragment format (F4F) for both live and on-demand media streaming. It was developed after the MSS and HLS standard. It uses the same structure that adjusts the video quality for improving the user's QoE by considering the client's network speed and processing power, using standard HTTP protocol infrastructures. HDS provides the best viewer streaming experience to a large number of end devices and platforms that support Adobe Flash software. Adobe developed two tools for preparing fragmented media streams: 1) File Packager, which is used to prepare on-demand media, and 2) Live Packager, which is used to prepare live RTMP streams. The two packagers are used to generate MP4 fragment files (F4F) and an XML-based manifest file (F4M) and optionally provide content protection.

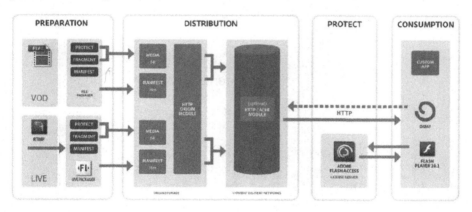

Figure 1.4. *Preparation, distribution, protection and consumption of HDS*

1.4.3. *Microsoft Smooth Streaming (MSS)*

Smooth Streaming was introduced by Microsoft in 2008 as part of its Silverlight architecture. It has core properties of adaptive video streaming. Video content is broken into small segments and delivered over HTTP. Multiple bitrates are provided to allow an end user to dynamically and seamlessly switch from one bitrate to another based on the network condition to increase its QoE. The resulting user experience is reliable and offers a consistent playback without stutter, buffering or congestion; in other words, it is smooth. MSS uses the ISO/IEC 14496-12 ISO Base Media File Format specification, also known as the MP4 file specification. MP4 is a lightweight container format with fewer overheads, which is used to deliver a series of segments for smooth video streaming. Smooth Streaming consists of two formats: the disk file format and the wire format. Normally, a full-length video is stored as a single file on the disk that is encoded with a specific bitrate. During the streaming, it is transferred as sequences of small fragments (segments or chunks). The disk file format defines the structure of continuous files on the disk, whereas the wire format defines the structure of each segment/chunk that is transferred from the server to the client. The file format of MSS is shown in Figure 1.5. The file structure starts with file-level metadata "*moov*" that represents the file, while the fragment boxes describe the fragment-level metadata ("*moof*") and the media data ("*mdat*"). The file structure ends with a $mfra$ index that helps in searching within the file.

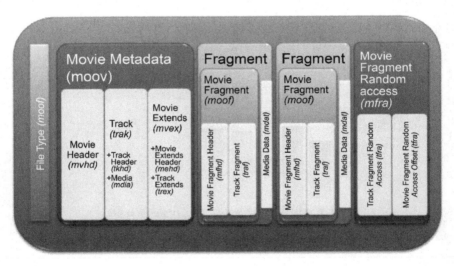

Figure 1.5. *File format of MSS [BOC 13]*

The web server searches the MP4 file to find a video fragment that is requested by the client player. The requested file fragment is sent to the client over the wire, hence the name "wire format". The format of the fragment is shown in Figure 1.6.

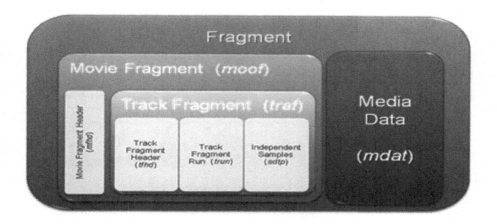

Figure 1.6. *Fragment format of MSS [BOC 13]*

1.4.4. *Apple's HTTP Live Streaming (HLS)*

Apple chose the MOV file format as its adaptive streaming technology, unlike the well-known ISO MPEG file format. It allows audio and video to be sent over HTTP from a simple web server for playing on different kinds of IOS-based end devices, such as iPod, iPad, iPhone, Apple TV and desktop Mac OS X computers. The Safari web browser is a client software that plays HTTP live streams using the tag. In HLS, the adaptive transport of video streaming is achieved by sending sequences of small files of video/audio that generally last 10 seconds, known as media segment files. Apple provides a free tool to generate the media segment and playlists (manifest file) for on-demand and live streams. The basic configuration architecture of HLS is shown in Figure 1.7. The server components (media encoder and segmenter) have the responsibility to take the input from the source media, encode them into the MPEG-2 transport stream (TS), and split them into a series of TS files that encapsulate both audio and video in a format that is suitable for delivery to an end-user device. The web server is the main part of the distribution component that accepts and responds to the client requests. The client software is responsible for generating appropriate media segment requests and downloading and reassembling them so that the media stream can playback in a continuous manner, in order to maintain a high user QoE.

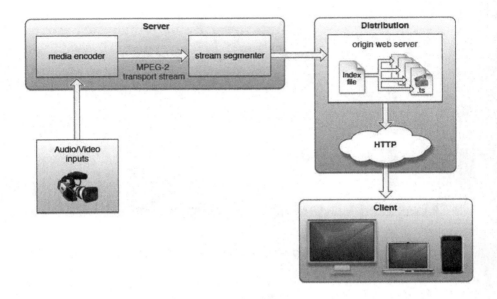

Figure 1.7. *Basic configuration architecture of HLS*

1.4.5. *MPEG's Dynamic Adaptive Streaming over HTTP (DASH)*

The Moving Picture Expert Group (MPEG) has developed many multimedia standards, including MPEG-2, MPEG-4, MPEG-7 and MPEG-21. Recently, the group developed a standard for streaming multimedia over the Internet (HTTP). This standard is known as MPEG-DASH or simply DASH. The format used by the DASH standard is similar to HDS, MSS and HLS, where the index files (manifest or playlist files) describe the order in which segments or chunks are downloaded and played for continuous media streaming. Figure 1.8 shows a simple DASH streaming scenario between an HTTP server and the DASH client. In this figure, the multimedia content is captured and stored on a server and delivered to the client using HTTP. The server contains two content parts: the first one is the Media Presentation Description (MPD), which describes a manifest file about the available contents, including various alternative formats, URL addresses and other characteristics; the second one is the segment part, which contains the actual multimedia bitstreams in the form of chunks, in single or multiple files.

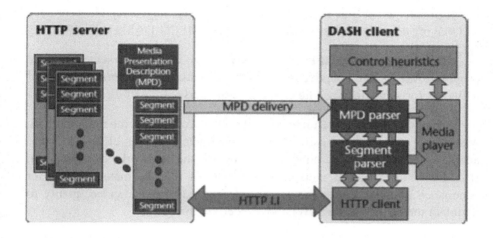

Figure 1.8. *Streaming scenario of DASH [SOD 11]*

To play the content, the DASH client first obtains the manifest or playlist file (i.e. MPD). The MPD can be delivered using HTTP or other transport methods, e.g. email, thumb drive, broadcast. Initially, the DASH client parses the MPD. Then, it learns about the following information: program timing, media-content availability, media types, resolutions, minimum and maximum bandwidth, and the existence of various encoded alternatives of multimedia components, accessibility features and required digital rights management (DRM), media component locations on the network and other content characteristics. After parsing the MPD, the DASH client selects the appropriate encoded segment and starts streaming the content by fetching the segments using HTTP GET requests.

The appropriate buffering allows for network throughput variations, and the client continues to fetch the successive segments and monitors the fluctuations in network bandwidth. Based on its measurement results, the client decides how to adapt according to the available bandwidth and then fetches the segments of different qualities (lower or higher bitrates) to avoid buffer starvation [SOD 11]. Buffering plays a vital role in enabling uninterrupted or smoothed streaming, which in turn improves the client's QoE. The DASH specification only defines the MPD and the segment formats. The delivery of the MPD and the media-encoding formats containing the segments, as well as the client behavior for fetching, adaptive heuristics and playing content, are not within the scope of MPEG-DASH [ISO 13].

Although there are well-known adaptive video methods, researchers have proposed various rate-adaptive methods that consider the dynamic behavior of networks for achieving specific goals from the perspective of distinct metrics.

Earlier, the sender-driven rate adaptation was considered the main method, where the sender/server estimated the parameters at the client side and adapted the video streaming according to the network condition. In [LAM 04], an adaptive method was proposed that estimated the buffer occupancy of the client at the server side and adapted the video quality to maintain the client's buffer level above a certain threshold.

However, rate-adaptive approaches have switched from sender-driven to receiver-driven, where a client decides to adopt the video streaming quality by monitoring its parameters and network conditions. In [LIU 11], the authors proposed a receiver-driven rate adaptation algorithm for video streaming over HTTP. The proposed method was evaluated by using the NS-2 simulator with the exponential and constant bitrate background traffic. The method detected the changes in network bandwidth by using a smoothed HTTP throughput measured based on the segment fetch time (SFT). The results showed that the proposed algorithm did not select the appropriate video quality, as it depicted fluctuation in video quality selection process because of dynamic network conditions. In [AKH 12], the authors highlighted the behavior of different adaptive players for HTTP video streaming to check their stability in different scenarios. In [JIA 14], the authors observed the HTTP-based adaptive streaming method in terms of fairness, efficiency and stability.

A receiver-driven rate adaptation algorithm was proposed in [MIL 12], where it estimated the network bandwidth, and based on the client buffer length, it chose an appropriate video quality. The authors evaluated the algorithm in different bandwidth scenarios, keeping the target buffer interval between 20 and 50 seconds. It was noted that a larger buffer length minimized the number of video quality shifts because the impact of instantaneous variation in network conditions was less with no impact of dropped frame rate.

A QoE-aware algorithm for video streaming based on DASH was discussed in [MOK 12]. The main idea of video delivery was to optimize the user-perceived QoE. The authors showed that frequent changes in video rate significantly degraded the user's QoE, and thus proposed to change the video rate step by step based on the available bandwidth.

A rate-adaptive algorithm based on bandwidth estimation for HTTP video streaming systems was proposed in [ZHO 12]. The authors proposed this new method for bandwidth estimation. Based on the past transmission history, the algorithm predicted the amount of data that the client could download during a certain interval. The authors evaluated the proposed algorithm in terms of stalling frequency with constant bitrate (CBR), and did not consider the impact of the sudden drop in bandwidth and dropped video frame metrics.

1.5. Scheduling and power-saving methods

Many factors directly or indirectly influence the performance of wireless networks and UEs. Among these performance metrics, scheduling scheme has gained greater importance in efficiently allocating radio resources among the UEs. The emerging and fastest growing multimedia services such as Skype, GTalk and interactive video gaming have created new challenges for wireless communication technologies, especially in terms of resource allocation and power optimization of UEs as both schemes have a high impact on system performance and user satisfaction. Efficient resources and power optimization are very important in the next-generation communication systems (e.g. 5G) because new multimedia services are more resource and power hungry. With more traffic flow in the downlink than in the uplink, resource allocation schemes in the downlink have become more important than those in the uplink.

1.5.1. *Scheduling methods*

Scheduling is a process of allocating physical radio resources among users, in order to fulfill the QoS requirements of multimedia services. The aim of a scheduling scheme is to maximize the overall system throughput while keeping fairness, delay and packet loss rate within the QoS requirements to satisfy end-users' QoE.

Users are generally classified based on their traffic characteristics such as real-time and non-real-time traffic. For real-time traffic (e.g. video, VoIP, gaming), scheduling must guarantee that QoS requirements are satisfied. The packet loss rate and delay play a vital role in user experience. Packets in real-time traffic must arrive at the user within a certain delay threshold, otherwise they are considered as lost or discarded. Scheduling decisions can be made based on the following parameters: MOS, QoS parameters, traffic type, channel quality indicator (CQI), resource allocation history and buffer status at both the eNodeB and UE.

The best channel quality indicator (BCQI) scheme allocates radio resources only to those UEs that have reported best channel conditions in the uplink through the CQI feedback to the corresponding eNodeB. Meanwhile, the UEs that suffer from bad channel conditions will never get radio resources [RAM 09]. As a result of the BCQI scheme, the overall system throughput increases, but UEs that are far away from the eNodeB will never get resources because of bad channel conditions. Thus, the BCQI scheme performs well in terms of throughput but poorly in terms of fairness among the UEs.

To overcome the fairness problem of the BCQI, the round robin (RR) scheme was developed. It distributes radio resources equally among the UEs to gain high fairness. As a result, the overall system throughput is degraded because it does not consider the channel conditions of UEs. To handle the constraints of high throughput and fairness, the proportional fair (PF) scheme was developed. This scheme uses an approach based on the trade-off between maximum achievable average throughputs and fairness.

A channel-adapted and buffer-aware packet scheduling scheme for the LTE communication system was proposed in [LIN 08]. This scheme makes scheduling decisions on QoS for real-time (RT) services, which are based on three elements: CQI and UE buffer status feedback on the uplink, treating RT and non-RT UE's traffic separately. However, this scheduling scheme does not consider the packet delay factor that can increase the packet loss rate and degrade user satisfaction.

A two-layer scheduling scheme was discussed in [BEH 08]. It maintains the fairness of radio resources and high throughput. However, the proposed scheme does not consider the packet delay and guaranteed bitrate (GBR) which are important parameters of an LTE system that influence the QoS and determine the overall user's QoE for the current service. In [DEL 10], an admission control and resource allocation packet scheduling scheme was presented. It combines the time-domain scheduling and frequency-domain scheduling to maximize the throughput while making sure that the user's delay never crosses the threshold value and that the user gets a minimum throughput to fulfill the QoS requirements. The QoS requirements are fulfilled by assigning more resources to those users that have critical delay and throughput (i.e. larger delay or minimum throughput). This proposed algorithm fulfills the QoS requirements of RT and non-RT traffic by considering the throughput and delay of each user, but it does not consider the channel conditions when allocating the resources to users.

A cross-layer resource allocation scheme for inter-cell interference coordination (ICIC) was proposed in [LU 11] for LTE networks. Game theory is used to solve an optimization problem, so that the total number of resource blocks in different cells is treated adequately; likewise, the convergence of the algorithm is guaranteed. This proposed method is evaluated using two scheduling methods, namely PF and modified largest weighted delay first (M-LWDF) with fixed power allocation; moreover, only the system throughput is considered as a performance metric. The cumulative distribution function (CDF) of the normalized user throughput is used to compare the fairness of the proposed cross-layer scheme with MAX C/I, RR and PF. The proposed method does not take into account the packet delay, GBR and other QoS parameters of LTE networks which influence the QoE of end users. In [SHI 12], the congestion exposure mechanism is used to feedback the real-time objective QoE information, as perceived by end-users, into the network. The authors proposed a new queue management technique based on QoE metrics. Our proposed method also uses the real-time feedback of UEs to make the scheduling decision.

1.5.2. *DRX power-saving method*

Researchers have used different methodologies to measure the overall power consumption of UEs. One way is to consider different factors that consist of hardware components (e.g. CPU, screen, SD card), wireless networks (e.g. WiFi, Bluetooth, ZigBee, 2G, 3G) and applications (e.g. video, voice) of the UE in order to measure overall energy consumption. Most of these approaches have been used to develop the power consumption model in order to estimate the power used by different components, as reported in

[CAR 10a, PER 09, BAL 09, XIA 10, ZHA 10, SHY 09, ANA 09] and [ZHO 10].

There are methods that use various states (idle, connected and power-saving) of the UE in order to develop the power consumption model [LAU 14]. In [LAU 13], the authors developed a power model for smartphones. The model considered the DRX operation along with cell bandwidth, screen and CPU power consumption using the simulator, but only in terms of the UE. The DRX method uses two cycles in the UMTS system [YAN 05], i.e. the DRX cycle for UE sleep (OFF) and the inactivity cycle (ON) for wake-up. The main purpose of DRX is to prolong the UE's battery life in order to avoid the quick draining of UE power. In the next-generation wireless communication system (i.e. 5G), the DRX power-saving mechanism will be an important technique to optimize the UE's battery life.

The increasing demand for high-speed data service and the dramatic expansion of network infrastructure have enormously increased energy consumption in wireless networks. Today, optimal energy consumption has become a major challenge. To overcome this challenge, different methods have been proposed for efficient energy use of different elements in wireless networks.

The DRX power-saving method is used in different wireless communication systems in order to prolong battery life by monitoring UE activities. It is based on a simple procedure: when there is no data transmission, the power can be saved by switching off the UE's wireless transceiver. During the sleep state of the UE, the DRX method considerably increases the packet delay.

The DRX mechanism of the UMTS was investigated in [YAN 05] using an analytical model, where only DRX functionality consists of two parameters: inactivity time and the DRX cycle, between the NodeB and the UE for saving the power of the UE. The effects of DRX cycles can be observed by considering the timers, queue length and packet waiting times. In [ZHO 08a], the authors presented an analytical model which proved that the LTE DRX mechanism has the ability to save more power than the UMTS DRX method [3GP 05].

The power-saving methods for two different WiMAX standards, i.e. IEEE 802.16e and IEEE 802.16m, were discussed in [CHO 12]. In their study, the authors highlighted important issues related to the power-saving mechanism in WiMAX networks and addressed several problems to improve its efficiency.

The influence of transmission time interval (TTI) sizes as well as the effects of LTE DRX Light and Deep Sleep modes on power consumption for voice and web traffic were evaluated in [FOW 11]. However, the authors of this study did not consider the effects of these parameters on QoS. In [BO 10], the DRX-aware scheduling was proposed, which included the DRX status as a scheduling decision parameter to reduce packet delay caused by the DRX sleep duration. The scheduling priority is directly proportional to its head-of-line packet delay with respect to the remaining active time before a UE enters into the sleep mode. In [FAN 08], a semi-persistent scheduling scheme for VoIP was developed using DRX. First, it organizes the UEs in the scheduling candidate set (SCS) based on the UE buffer information at the eNodeB, the DRX status and the persistent resource allocation pattern. Then, it calculates the priority metric for the UEs in the SCS by first favoring the UEs that require retransmissions and then the UEs whose packet delay of unsent packet in the eNodeB buffer is close to the delay threshold. Both schemes presented in [BO 10] and [FAN 08] use the DRX mechanism to optimize power usage and offer solutions to the problems caused by the sleep interval of increased packet delay and packet loss. However, both studies did not consider the GBR requirement of UEs.

In [AHO 09], the performance of the DRX mechanism was evaluated in terms of DRX cycle lengths and associated timer values by observing their effect on VoIP traffic services over the High-Speed Downlink Packet Access (HSDPA) network. However, the UE's battery life might be a key limiting factor in providing satisfactory user experience. The results showed that a longer DRX cycle saves more UE power, but VoIP capacity over HSDPA can be compromised when selecting unsuitable DRX parameters.

In [ZHO 13b], the authors presented a semi-Markov chain model to analyze the impact of the DRX mechanism in LTE networks using the machine-type communication (MTC) traffic, while in [JIN 12], the authors proposed a method for modeling the DRX mechanism in LTE wireless networks using the Poisson traffic. Similarly, in [FOW 12], an analytical model was used to study the influence of fixed and adjustable DRX cycle mechanisms in LTE networks with the bursty packet data traffic using a semi-Markov process. However, none of these methods proposed in

[ZHO 13b, JIN 12] and [FOW 12] considered QoS characteristics such as fair resource allocation, packet loss rate and throughput which can badly affect the DRX mechanism in LTE networks.

The impact of the LTE DRX Light Sleep mechanism on QoS was examined in [MUS 12] using the VoIP traffic model. However, the study only evaluated the performance of the LTE DRX Light Sleep cycle and not the Deep Sleep cycle. In [JHA 12], DRX optimization was performed for the mobile Internet application by considering the DRX inactivity timer and the DRX cycle length with two users. This method was evaluated with only two users, and did not consider the impact on other QoS parameters such as fairness, throughput, packet loss rate and GBR requirement for RT traffic.

2

Methodologies for Subjective Video Streaming QoE Assessment

In the previous chapter, we reviewed the literature on studies related to this work. This and the following two chapters make three main contributions. This chapter presents the first contribution referred to as subjective methods for evaluating the user's QoE using video streaming. In this chapter, we describe two important subjective methods: controlled environment and uncontrolled environment methods. First, the two methods are used to collect QoE datasets in the form of a Mean Opinion Score (MOS). Then, the dataset is used to analyze the correlation between QoS and QoE.

2.1. Introduction

Service providers are faced with the challenge of assessing the perceived Quality of Experience (QoE) for multimedia services. The user's QoE of video services is generally measured in a completely controlled environment (e.g. experimental testbed) because it provides the freedom to easily measure the impact of controlled network parameters. However, it is hard to assess the user-perceived Quality of Service (QoS) in a real-time uncontrolled environment due to the time-varying characteristics of network parameters. Crowdsourcing is a technique for measuring the user's QoE at the client side in an uncontrolled environment.

This chapter presents the methodologies to assess the QoE for video services. It is important to investigate how different factors contribute to the

QoE with respect to video streaming delivery over dynamic networks. The important parameters that influence the QoE are network parameters, video characteristics, terminal characteristics and users' profiles. This chapter describes two important subjective methods that are used to collect QoE datasets in the form of a MOS.

In a controlled environment, subjective laboratory experiments are first conducted to collect QoE datasets in the form of a MOS. The impacts of different factors are then evaluated using video services, and users' quality perception data are stored in the datasets. The collected datasets are used to analyze the correlation between QoS and QoE for video services. Machine learning methods are used to classify a QoE dataset that is collected using a real testbed experiment. We evaluated six classifiers to determine the most suitable one for analyzing the QoS and QoE correlation.

The analysis of users' profiles provides vital information, which can help service providers understand users' behavior and expectations in order to manage their resources efficiently. The information can also be used to investigate the influence of different QoS parameters on users' profiles to achieve the best QoE for multimedia video services. The comprehensive study of users' profiles from the perspective of different factors helps network service providers understand end-users' behavior and expectations.

In an uncontrolled environment, crowdsourcing is used to measure the user-perceived QoE of online video streaming in real time. The tool also measures important real-time QoS network parameters (packet loss, delay, jitter and throughput), retrieves system information (memory, processing power, etc.) and other properties of the end-user's system. The proposed approach provides the opportunity to explore the user's quality perception in a wider and more realistic domain.

2.2. Metrics affecting the QoE

QoE is very subjective by nature because of its relationship with the user's point of view and its own concept of "good quality". The ability to measure the QoE would give network operators some sense of the contribution of the network's performance to the overall customer satisfaction, in terms of reliability, availability, scalability, speed, accuracy and efficiency. First, it is necessary to identify precisely the factors that affect the QoE, and then to define methods for measuring these factors. We categorize these factors into three types, as described below.

2.2.1. *Network parameters*

QoE is influenced by QoS parameters that are highly dependent on network elements. The important factors are packet loss rate, jitter and delay. The impact of each individual or combined factors can lead to blocking, blurriness or even blackouts with quality degradation of video streaming at different levels.

2.2.1.1. *Packet loss*

Packet losses directly affect the quality of video presented to end-users. They occur due to network congestion and late arrival of packets at application buffers. When packet loss occurs, the video decoder cannot properly decode the video stream. This results in the degradation of video quality.

2.2.1.2. *Jitter*

Jitter is another important QoS parameter that has a great impact on video quality. It is defined as the variance of packet arrival times at the end-user buffer. It occurs when packets travel on different network paths to reach the same destination. It causes jerkiness and frozen video screens.

However, the effects of jitter can be nullified or reduced to some extent by adding a large receiving buffer at the end-user to delay the play-out time of the video. Nevertheless, when a packet arrives out of order, i.e. after the buffering time expires, this packet is discarded by the application. In this context, jitter has the same influence as packet loss [VEN 11].

2.2.1.3. *Delay*

Delay is defined as the amount of time taken by the packet to reach the destination. It has a direct influence on user perception when watching the video. When the delay exceeds a certain threshold, it results in freezing and lost blocks of the video. The threshold value of delay varies according to the nature of the multimedia service.

2.2.2. *Video characteristics*

The characteristics of the video are defined in terms of frame and resolution rates, codecs and content types. The impact of reducing the bitrate of video streaming services according to the available bandwidth on user satisfaction is discussed in [JAN 10]. Video content types can also influence user perception. For example, when watching "interesting" video content, a user will be more tolerant and its low quality will not have as much influence on the user's experience as when watching boring content. In [MCC 04], it has been found that when users show enough interest in the video content, they accept even an extremely low frame rate. In that study, the participants were those who were interested in soccer. The participants gave a very high accepance rate (80%), although they watched a video with only 6 frames per second. This result clearly shows that if there is a sufficient interest in the topic, then the human visual system can tolerate relatively gross interruptions and very low-quality video streaming.

An uncompressed video requires a large amount of storage and bandwidth to be streamed over a network. Therefore, a large number of video codecs have been developed (H.262, H.263, H.264, WVID, WMV3, etc.) to compress the video effectively and efficiently in order to maintain an acceptable quality of videos. Each codec has its own standard way to compress the video contents, thereby providing various video quality levels. The quality levels of video codecs explain the important effect of codecs on user perception.

Generally, the user's interest is measured by monitoring the access frequency of a specific video (e.g. on the Internet). However, this approach is not suitable to measure the user's interest and preference for the video content. The optimal method to measure the user's interest in a specific video is to record the number of clicks and time spent watching. The total time that the user spends in watching the video provides significant information about the user's interest.

2.2.3. *Terminal types*

Electronic devices are expanding rapidly with new advancements in the telecommunication industry, offering a large number of products for modern multimedia services. These new-generation devices come in different sizes and features such as processing power, advanced functionality, usage and many other aspects. However, these terminal devices may have a problem with the aspect ratio and video content available to the end-user device. Internet browsers have the ability to provide relevant information about device properties such as screen resolution, operating system and browser type. These key data can be used to determine the impact of various system parameters on the end-user's QoE. The impact of different terminal devices on the end-user's QoE can be analyzed using a set of different target end-user devices. Terminal devices can be classified into three categories: computers, television and smart mobile devices. These terminal devices can influence user satisfaction while using video streaming services. For example, it would be pointless to send HD video streaming to a low processing terminal with a small screen.

2.2.3.1. Television (TV)

The TV market has witnessed a tremendous growth. Companies are offering different TV models with amazing features. These features can be summarized as follows:

– screen size (40, 65 inch);

– size (WxHxD, e.g. 1062x700x46.9 mm);

– HD format (720p, 1080i, 1080p);

– color system;

– TV type (LED, Plasma);

– 3D capable;

– support for tablet, smart phone and other devices.

2.2.3.2. Computers

Currently, many different categories of computer are available in the market. It has become hard for people to select the perfect computer because each computer provides different features. In fact, it is difficult to select the right model as it all depends on computer use to achieve the desired goal. Some users prefer good performance while others give high priority to portability. For laptop devices, features that should be considered are battery life, gaming performance and screen quality. The important elements of a computer can be summarized as follows:

– screen size (e.g. 17 inches);

– thin screen;

– processing power;

– 3D graphics card with its own memory and processing power;

– operating system;

– memory power.

2.2.3.3. Smart mobile devices

Recent advances in research have led to the development of a large variety of smart mobile devices, which are powerful enough to support a wide range of multimedia traffic (e.g. video streaming, VoIP, multiplayer interactive gaming) and also legacy mobile services (e.g. voice, SMS, MMS). These new multimedia applications require high data rates and processing power to enhance the end-user's experience. The important elements of smart mobile devices can be summarized as follows:

– display and size (800 x 1280 pixels, 10.1 inches);

– processing power (Quad-core 1.4 GHz);

– memory size (up to 64 GB);

– stereo sound quality;

– video output support;

– wireless connectivity (e.g. WiFi, GSM, UMTS, LTE/LTE-A);

– battery life.

2.2.4. Psychological factors

QoS network parameters (packet loss, delay and jitter) are used to ensure service guarantees in order to maximize the application's performance. However, QoS fails to determine an important element, i.e. user perception about the current service because prediction of the user's behavior is hard. Therefore, network service providers must take into account a large number of parameters and metrics that directly reflect the user's emotional behavior, in order to determine the adequate quality level of multimedia services.

For a specific multimedia service, user perception varies from one individual to another. The estimation of the quality level depends on many factors which are related to an individual's preferences and the surrounding environment. Some of these factors are classified as follows:

– user's characteristics (age, sex, background knowledge, language, task familiarity);

– situation characteristics and viewing conditions (noisy space, number of simultaneous users, at home, in a car);

– user's behavior and his/her attention to the video being played.

2.3. Machine learning classification methods

We use machine learning (ML) methods to classify a preliminary QoE dataset that is collected from a laboratory experiment, as described in section 2.5.1. Based on this dataset, we determine whether ML methods can help build an accurate and objective QoE model that correlates low-level parameters with high-level quality. We thus evaluated six classifiers to determine the most suitable one for analyzing the QoS and QoE correlation.

ML is concerned with the design and development of programs and algorithms that have the ability to automatically improve their performance based on their own experience over time or on earlier data provided by other programs. The general functions of ML are training, recognition, generalization, adaptation, improvement and intelligibility. There are two types of ML: unsupervised learning and supervised learning. Unsupervised learning refers to finding the hidden structure in unlabeled data in order to classify it into meaningful categories. On the other hand, supervised learning assumes that the category structure or hierarchy of the database is already known. It requires a set of labeled classes to return a function that maps the database to predefined class labels. In other words, supervised learning is the search for algorithms that reason from externally supplied instances to produce general hypotheses. It makes predictions about future instances in order to build a concise model that represents the data distribution. In our case, we consider supervised learning, focusing on classification methods due to the discrete nature of our datasets. We applied six ML classification methods to our datasets, which include naive Bayes, support vector machines, k-nearest neighbors, decision trees, random forests and neural networks.

2.3.1. Naive Bayes

The naive Bayes (NB) classifier is a probabilistic model that uses the joint probabilities of terms and categories to estimate the probabilities of categories given in a test document. The naive part of the classifier comes from the simplifying assumption that all terms are conditionally independent of each other in a given category. Because of this independence assumption, the parameters for each term can be learned separately; therefore, this simplifies and speeds up computation operations [COR 10].

2.3.2. Support vector machines

Support vector machine (SVM) is a very powerful classification method that is used to solve a two-class pattern recognition problem. It analyzes the data and identifies patterns in order to make a classification. The idea here is to find the optimal separating hyperplane between two classes, by maximizing the margin between the closest points of these two classes. SVM classifies data based on whether or not it can be linearly separable in its origin domain. The simple linear SVM can be used if the data is linearly separable. When the data is non-separable in its original domain through the hyperplane, then it can be projected in a higher-dimensional Hilbert space. The data can be linearly separable in a higher-dimensional space using a kernel function [ZHA 04].

2.3.3. K-nearest neighbors

The k-nearest neighbour (k-NN) method is an instance-based ML method and considered to be very simple compared with other ML classification methods. Among the methods of supervised statistical pattern recognition, the k-NN method often performs better than other methods. The prior supposition of distribution is not required when the training sample is drawn. It works in a very simple and straightforward way: to classify any new test sample, it compares the new test sample with all the other samples in the training set.

The category labels of these neighbors are used to estimate the category of the test sample. In other words, it first calculates the distance between the new test sample and the nearest training sample and then this point will determine the classification of the sample [ISL 07].

2.3.4. Decision tree

Decision tree (DT) is a method used to create a model to predict the value of a target variable based on several input variables. The structure of DT consists of the following elements: (1) internal nodes, which test an attribute, (2) branches, which correspond to attribute values and (3) leaf nodes, which assign a classification. Instances are classified by starting at the root node and, based on the feature values, the tree is sorted down to a leaf node. It is a simple classifier that can efficiently classify new data and compactly store them. It has the ability to reduce complexity and automatically select features. DT has a built-in property to estimate suitable features that separate objects representing different classes. The information about the prediction of classification can be easily interpreted, thanks to its tree structure. Finally, the accuracy of DT is less affected by user-defined factors when compared with the k-NN classifier [PAL 02].

2.3.5. Random forest

Random forest (RF) is an ensemble classifier that uses multiple models of several DTs to obtain a better prediction performance. It creates many classification trees and a bootstrap sample technique is used to train each tree from the set of training data. This method only searches for a random subset of variables in order to obtain a split at each node. For the classification, the input vector is fed to each tree in the RF and each tree votes for a class. Finally, the RF chooses the class with the highest number of votes. It has the ability to handle larger input datasets when compared with other methods [AUN 09].

2.3.6. Neural networks

A neural network (NNT) is a structure of a large number of units (neurons) linked together in a pattern of connections. The interconnections are used to send signals from one neuron to the other. The calculation in NNTs is based on the transfer of information between basic units of computation. The possibilities of each one are small but their interconnection allows a complex overall calculation. The behavior of an NNT is determined by its architecture: number of cells, how they are connected and the weights assigned to each connection. The connection between two neurons is characterized by the connection weight, which measures the degree of influence of the first neuron on the second one. The weight is updated during a training period. This method has the ability to solve multivariate nonlinear problems. Its performance is degraded when it is applied to a large number of training datasets [AUN 09].

2.4. Experimental environment for QoE assessment

In general, the QoE assessment is done by using the subjective method because it matches the real perception of users while using a service. Generally, two distinct approaches are available to collect QoE datasets: the crowdsourcing environment approach and the controlled environment approach. In crowdsourcing, the video testing task is assigned to a large number of anonymous users who can participate from different regions of the world from their own environment. The proposed crowdsourcing approach is presented in section 2.7. In parallel to the crowdsourcing approach, there is an orthogonal approach in which the experimental environment is totally controlled.

2.4.1. *Controlled environment approach*

The controlled environment approach is a laboratory test environment, which is specially designed to fix the environmental factors that can influence the user's viewing experience. The International Telecommunication Union Telecommunication Standardization Sector (ITU-T) has made the recommendation to set up the laboratory test and describe the criteria for selecting the participants to conduct the test. The ITU-T recommendation [INT 08] has provided guidelines to conduct subjective tests in a controlled environment, including the selection of participants who represent the users of a service. To obtain the subjective notation according to the ITU-T recommendation [INT 09], participants should be non-experts, in the sense that they should not be directly concerned with image or video quality as part of their normal work. This approach has the following advantages:

– the testing environment can be totally controlled;

– the influence of an individual parameter can be easily monitored;

– participants from different backgrounds, professions, age groups, etc. can be selected independently.

The controlled environment approach has some limitations to assessing the performance of QoE:

– it is a time-consuming test;

– the number of participants willing to spend their time in the laboratory test and express their perception of quality for the video service is limited.

– it is an expensive approach in terms of buying special equipment and apparatuses to conduct the test.

– it is difficult to set up a particular laboratory environment to resemble the real-world environment.

2.4.2. *Crowdsourcing environment approach*

The crowdsourcing environment is an alternative to the laboratory testing approach for assessing the QoE of video services. In this approach, a testing task (e.g. video quality) is assigned to a large number of anonymous users who can participate from different regions of the world via the Internet. It is an efficient approach in which collected datasets represent the opinion of a large number of participants on their quality experience. This approach has the following advantages:

– provides an open environment that represents the real user's QoE while using the service;

– helps in collecting a large amount of QoE data for analysis;

– allows the remote participation of a large number of anonymous participants;

– collects QoE parameters in real time;

– completes the testing task within a short period of time;

– saves the cost of setting up a real-world environment and expensive equipment.

This approach also has some disadvantages in assessing the performance of QoE:

– provides an uncontrolled environment that represents the real user's environment;

– has different environments for each participant;

– requires installation of software at the end-user's device;

– requires description or training for each participant in order to conduct the testing task.

2.5. Testbed experiment

We conducted a testbed experiment to analyze the impact of distinct parameters on user-perceived quality of video streaming. A subjective test was undertaken by 45 participants. The participants watched the video streaming and rated the quality of different videos.

In this testbed experiment, QoS parameters (packet loss, jitter and delay) were varied in a fully controlled manner. Furthermore, their influence on user perception was recorded in the form of a MOS. In addition, another parameter was considered, namely conditional loss. Conditional loss reflects the loss probability of the next packet, given that the current packet has already been lost. As most real-time applications exhibit a certain tolerance against infrequent packet losses, this metric helps in concentrating losses on a single part of the sequence, which makes the losses occasional. The relevant parameters and their selected values in our experiment are given in Table 2.1.

Parameters	Value
Delay	0ms, 30ms, 60ms, 100ms, 120ms
Jitter	0ms, 4ms, 8ms, 16ms, 32ms
Packet loss	0%–5% (in 0.5% increments)
Conditional loss	0%, 30%, 60%, 90%

Table 2.1. *QoS metrics*

In this experiment, we considered users' participation according to the recommendation of ITU-R Rec. BT.500-11 [INT 09]. To obtain a subjective notation according to this recommendation, participants should be non-experts, in the sense that they should not be directly concerned with image or video quality as part of their normal work. Users' characteristics were also stored for analysis, including users' profiles such as age, gender, familiarity with video streaming and interest in video contents, as presented in Table 2.2. End-users' devices included mobile, tablet, notebook, Samsung HD screen and Dell desktops with Intel core duo processor and a display size of 1024×740. Mozilla Firefox was used as the web navigator.

Users' profiles	Values
Age	18–30 years
Gender	Male, female
Familiarity with video streaming	Rarely, weekly, daily
Interest in video contents	Interested, not interested

Table 2.2. *Users' characteristics*

A total of 25 HD and non-HD video streams were selected for this experiment, with different motion complexities (high, alternating and low), but with the same frame rate (25 frames per second) and video codec (H.264). These videos were related to different fields of interest (e.g. politics, sports, news, social life, commercial ads and animated cartoons). In our experimental analysis, we used NetEm as a network emulator to control the QoS parameters. This tool can emulate the properties of wide area networks (WAN); its functionalities have been evaluated in [JUR 11].

2.5.1. *Experimental setup*

Generally, the laboratory experimental setup consists of three important elements: a video streaming server, a video client and the network emulator (NetEm), which emulates a core and cloud network. This basic experimental setup is illustrated in Figure 2.1. Traffic flows between the server and the client are regulated via the network emulator. The emulator introduces artificial delay, jitter and packet loss within a dedicated connection. As shown in Figure 2.1, the client sends a request message to the video server and obtains the requested video via NetEm. When the video ends, the client provides their feedback as the perceived video quality in the form of a MOS, which is stored in an SQL database.

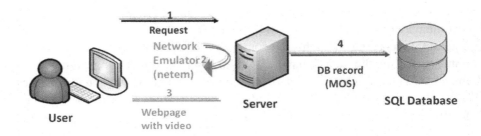

Figure 2.1. *Example: basic testbed setup*

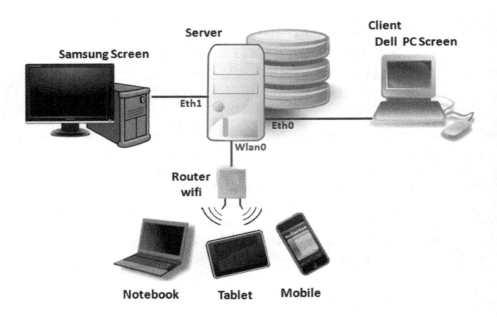

Figure 2.2. *Experimental setup*

Our experimental setup is shown in Figure 2.2. We stored 25 videos at the server side where the client could reach them through a private website. The client device (either wireless or wired) can connect to the website to read the description of the experiment and provide personal information (e.g. age, gender). Users were unaware of the QoS parameter settings on the videos, and they were asked to rate the perceived quality (in the form of a MOS) after watching each video. The client side consisted of different devices which include desktop devices, tablet and mobile, while the streaming server and the shaper (NetEm) were configured on a Linux OS. The resultant QoE of each video was stored in the database in the form of a MOS.

A total of 45 users participated in this experiment, of which 20 were female and 25 were male. Most of them were in the age group of 18–30. We collected a total of 1125 (25*45) samples in our database; in other words, there were 1125 different combinations of all settled parameters, with each combination associated with a MOS value. However, this number was reduced after averaging repeated lines and eliminating the parasitic ones.

The laboratory-based test is time-consuming but it can easily investigate the influence of each factor on a desired service. In our experiment, we collected the suitable dataset to investigate the impact of different factors on users' QoE. The number of participants and amount of video content in our testbed was good when compared with [MOK 11] which used only one video clip and 10 participants to conduct the laboratory test.

2.5.2. *Data analysis using ML methods*

Datasets obtained from the controlled experiment are first processed and cleaned to remove any parasitic information. The datasets are then ready for data analysis. We considered nine parameters as inputs to our ML tool: gender, viewing frequency, interest, delay, jitter, loss, conditional loss, motion complexity and resolution. We performed a four-fold cross-validation to estimate the error rate efficiently and without bias as follows: one sub-sample was used as the testing data and three sub-samples were used as the training data. This procedure was repeated four times, with each of the four sub-samples used exactly once as the testing data. All the results were averaged to obtain a single estimation. The modeling process was performed using six ML classification models to determine the best model. As mentioned earlier, these six classification models are NB, 4-NN, SMV, DT, RF and NNT. We used the WEKA tool to run these different algorithms on the dataset. This tool provides information about the classification model generated as well as its performance and imperfection with detailed averaged statistical data. We considered the mean absolute error rate to compare the error rate between the different models. The results are shown in Figure 2.3.

Among the classification models, DT showed the minimum absolute error rate (0.126), followed by RF (0.136). SVM showed the highest error rate (0.26). Therefore, the results indicate that the DT and RF models are most reliable on the current datasets.

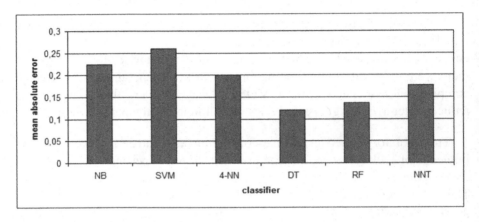

Figure 2.3. *Mean absolute error rate of the six classification methods*

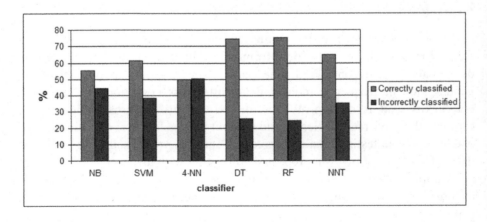

Figure 2.4. *Instance classification*

To choose the best model, we also performed an instance classification test on the six algorithms, in terms of the number of correctly classified instances. Figure 2.4 shows that two methods correspond to the best classification: RF with 74.8% of correctly classified instances, followed by DT with 74% of correctly classified data. The worst model is 4-NN with 49% of correctly classified instances. Again, these results indicate that DT and RF are the best models on our datasets.

To find more details about the models and their classification errors, we compared the efficiency of the DT and RF models. The efficiency of these models was evaluated using their statistical analysis data, as presented in Table 2.3.

Model	TP	FP	Precision	Recall	F-measure
RF	0.753	0.078	0.752	0.753	0.752
DT	0.743	0.084	0.748	0.743	0.745

Table 2.3. *Weighted average of the RF and DT models*

We considered five statistical metrics to compare the performance of the DT and RF models: true positive (TP), false positive (FP), precision, recall and F-measure.

– TP: occurs when a statistical test rejects a true hypothesis. The best value for this measure is 1;

– FP: a false value means rejecting the hypothesis. The value for this measure should be close to 0, which means the model works well;

– Precision: the probability when a (randomly selected) retrieved result is relevant:

Precision = TP/ (TP+FP);

– Recall: the probability when a (randomly selected) relevant document is retrieved in a search:

Recall = TP / (TP+FN);

– F-measure: a measure of test accuracy, an F1 score reaches its best value at 1 and, conversely, in the worst case its value is 0:

F-measure = 2∗ (Precision ∗ Recall) / (Precision + Recall).

The results of a classification can be negative or positive. If the results of the test correspond to reality, then we consider that a correct decision has been made. However, if the result of the test does not correspond to reality, then it implies that an error has occurred. According to these metrics, we conclude in Table 2.3 that the RF model is slightly more suitable than the DT model for analyzing the QoS and QoE correlation.

2.6. Analysis of users' profiles

The subjective dataset is used to analyze users' profiles that provide vital information to service providers, which helps them to understand users' behavior and expectations to manage their resources efficiently. The comprehensive study of users' profiles provides significant insights into all metrics that influence the QoE (network parameters and video characteristics). Although wireless and wired networks have different infrastructure aspects (reliability, availability, etc.), the analysis and evaluation of users' profiles are equally important for both the networks. Our analytical study provides an opportunity to network service providers to obtain high user satisfaction by providing a service level that matches customers' usage patterns and expectations. We consider two cases that provide important information on users' profiles and other parameters.

2.6.1. *Case 1: interesting and non-interesting video contents*

In this case, we consider video contents associated with the user's interest and non-interest. We observe how QoS parameters influence the user's interest in the video content. Here, we consider only the dataset that has a MOS equal to or greater than 3 because users are satisfied with these scores. Figure 2.5(a) compares the impact of delay on interesting and non-interesting video contents. It shows that when the delay is very low (0 ms), a large number of users show high satisfaction in watching the video content with a high MOS. When the value of delay is increased (above 30 ms), the number of users watching the video content starts decreasing quickly. Therefore, these results show that network service providers should keep the delay below 30 ms for video streaming. This delay threshold will help network service providers obtain high user satisfaction along with efficient utilization of network resources. Figure 2.5(b) presents the influence of packet loss rates on interesting and non-interesting video contents. It is important to note that the number of dataset records categorized as "non-interesting" is much less than that categorized as "interesting". The results indicate that when network operators target high user satisfaction, they must provide a low packet loss rate (at least less than 1%).

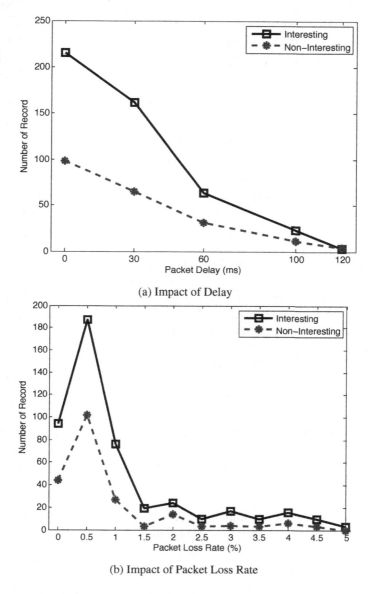

(a) Impact of Delay

(b) Impact of Packet Loss Rate

Figure 2.5. *Interesting and non-interesting video contents*

2.6.2. *Case 2: frequency, HD and non-HD video content*

In this case, we consider three important parameters that represent end-users' behavior and expectations while watching video streaming. We analyze the datasets that relate to the frequency of watching HD and non-HD video content. Again, we consider only the datasets that have a MOS equal to or greater than 3. Our analysis is based on QoS parameters, namely delays and loss rates.

Figure 2.6(a) shows the impact of delay on users who watch non-HD and HD video content rarely. It shows that occasional viewers are less sensitive to delay when watching non-HD video contents, but more sensitive to delay when watching HD videos. A small number of viewers are recorded for HD video streaming when compared with rare video viewers. Therefore, network service providers should keep a low delay to achieve high user satisfaction of HD video streaming.

Figure 2.6(b) shows the impact of packet loss rates on users who watch non-HD and HD video contents rarely. In the case of non-HD video streaming, a large number of users tolerate a packet loss rate up to 1%, but the number decreases with increasing packet loss rates. However, in the case of HD video streaming, users are more sensitive to packet loss rates and thus will not tolerate a packet loss rate greater than 0.5%.

Figure 2.7(a) shows the impact of delay on users who watch non-HD and HD video contents on a weekly basis. The results show that these users are less sensitive to delay when compared with users who rarely watch non-HD video streaming. The results show that the small number of users watching HD video streaming corresponds to that of occasional video viewers. The users who watch non-HD and HD video streaming weekly are more tolerant than those who watch rarely.

Figure 2.7(b) shows the impact of packet loss rates on users who watch non-HD and HD video contents weekly. Non-HD video content has a larger number of viewers than HD video content. In the case of non-HD videos, a large number of users watch video contents when the packet loss rate is below 0.5%, but the number decreases when the rate exceeds 1%. On the other hand, weekly viewers of HD video contents are sensitive to packet loss rates. These results indicate that network service providers must optimize their networks to keep the packet loss rate equal to or less than 1% to achieve high user satisfaction.

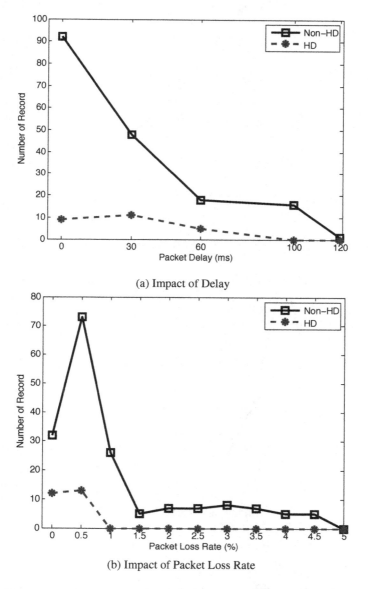

(a) Impact of Delay

(b) Impact of Packet Loss Rate

Figure 2.6. *Occasional viewers of HD and non-HD video contents*

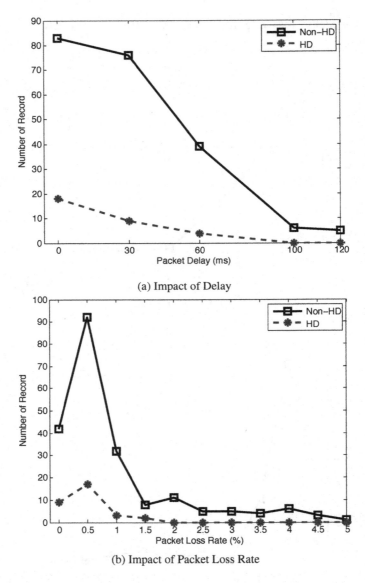

(a) Impact of Delay

(b) Impact of Packet Loss Rate

Figure 2.7. *Weekly viewers of HD and non-HD video contents*

Figure 2.8(a) shows the impact of delay on users who watch non-HD and HD video contents on a daily basis. It can be seen that a large number of viewers fall in this category. In both the cases, the results show that daily video viewers are to some extent less sensitive to delay than occasional or weekly viewers of the video.

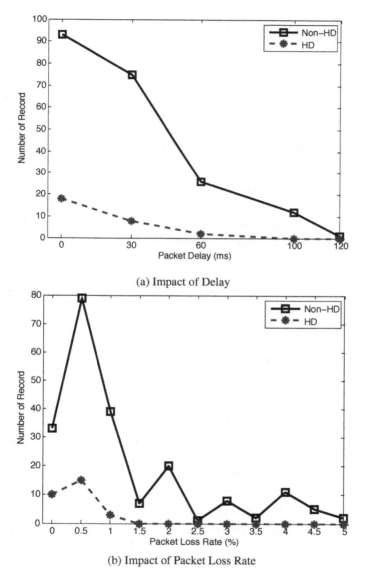

(a) Impact of Delay

(b) Impact of Packet Loss Rate

Figure 2.8. *Daily viewers of HD and non-HD video contents*

Figure 2.8(b) shows the impact of packet loss rates on users who watch non-HD and HD video content on a daily basis. A large number of viewers fall in this category. The results show that users are more tolerant to packet loss rates when compared with occasional or weekly video viewers. By contrast, HD video viewers are less tolerant to packet loss rates and their small number corresponds to that of weekly video viewers.

It can be observed that users are more tolerant when watching interesting video content than when watching non-interesting videos. However, users are more sensitive to delay and packet loss rates when viewing HD video contents but more tolerant when viewing non-HD videos.

2.7. Crowdsourcing method

Two subjective testing approaches can be used for assessing the QoE of video services: controlled environment and crowdsourcing environment. Crowdsourcing has emerged as an efficient method for performing subjective testing in the real world (the user's own environment). In crowdsourcing, users can participate remotely from any region of the world by using their own devices.

2.7.1. *Crowdsourcing framework*

Living laboratory is a new concept that has been used in different research fields, with a focus on user experience. It tries to bring the laboratory to volunteers in a realistic context. The goal of our proposed work is to assess the QoE in real time by building a larger dataset. This objective can be achieved by developing a tool that uses the Internet as the simulation platform and provides the opportunity of remote participation to users. The crowdsourcing framework tool is based on two parts: first, it detects the video on the website and, when the video ends, it asks the user about the perceived quality of video streaming. Second, it measures and stores real-time factors that influence the user's QoE, e.g. QoS network parameters, terminal device characteristics, etc.

The framework tool records the degree of user satisfaction in the feedback form while using video services on the Internet. The feedback form is shown in Figure 2.12. The proposed framework tool is tested by using the YouTube web portal, which has the largest cloud network for video delivery and is considered one of the most prominent video streaming websites. According to [KRI 11], 14.6 billion videos per day were viewed on YouTube in May 2010. The framework tool detects the presence of a YouTube video on a web page and automatically adds a button for the user to click when he/she is unhappy about video quality. The plug-in tool also stores QoE values, which are used to build a large dataset of heterogeneous users, devices and situations. Figure 2.9 shows the framework structure in which remote users participate via an IP network (Internet).

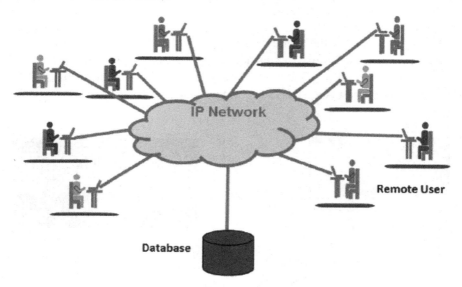

Figure 2.9. *Crowdsourcing framework*

The framework setup consists of the following items:

– A Firefox plug-in is developed and installed on end-users' devices to run the real-time experiment. In particular, the plug-in detects the presence of a video on a web page and automatically adds a button for the user to click when he/she is unhappy about video quality, as shown in Figure 2.11.

– A large number of remote volunteers are invited to watch video sequences online on their devices. Users can watch any video on the YouTube platform.

– Each video can have different characteristics and various realistic QoS parameters.

– Terminal properties and system processing data are measured while viewing each video and stored in a local database.

– Users rate the quality of video (MOS) according to their perception during and at the end of the video playback.

– All feedback information is stored in the database for future analysis of QoE parameters.

2.7.2. *Framework architecture*

Figure 2.10 shows the architecture of our framework. It is based on two major modules: a Firefox extension and a Java application. First, all information is stored in a local database at the user's terminal device. Then, these collected datasets are transferred to a remote server.

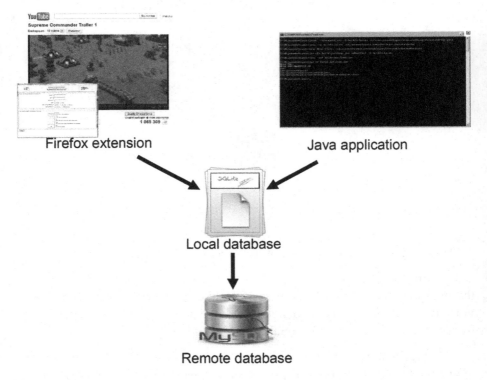

Figure 2.10. *Crowdsourcing framework architecture*

2.7.3. *Firefox extension*

The Firefox extension is developed in JavaScript, which is a prototype-based and object-oriented scripting language widely used in web development. It is a complement to XML in the Firefox extension, in order to enhance, enrich and improve the graphic interface of an application. The main functions of our Firefox extension are as follows:

– it analyzes the loaded web page. If a YouTube web page (e.g. YouTube) is found, then it inserts a button at the bottom of the online video, as shown in Figure 2.11;

– the "QoE Feedback" menu item is added under the "Tools" menu in the Firefox menu;

– a feedback form will open on clicking the button, in order to take the feedback from the user and store the information in the local database, as shown in Figure 2.12;

– it also stores information about video duration, video ID, video content type, operating system version and screen resolution.

Figure 2.11. *Framework implementation*

In the subjective approach, the most common question is to ask the user's opinion about the video streaming quality followed by other relevant questions for analyzing the user's QoE. In our framework, the user's feedback form is used for this purpose, as shown in Figure 2.12. It comprises the following items: name, age, profession, sex (male or female), video viewing frequency (rarely, weekly or daily), video content (interesting or non-interesting) and user quality experience (MOS).

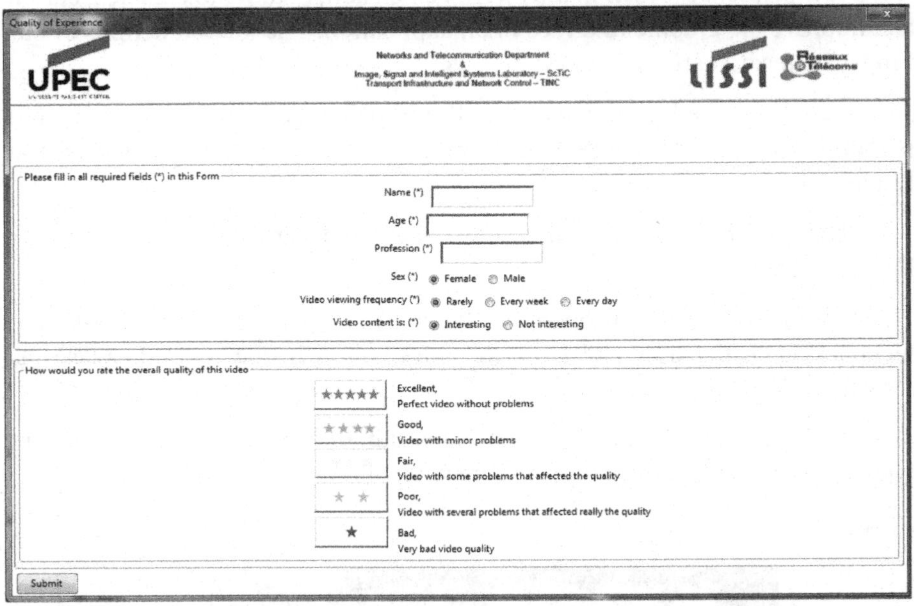

Figure 2.12. *User's feedback form*

We present the framework test only on the YouTube website; however, our Firefox extension is also compatible with DailyMotion and TF1 (French live video streaming content provider). In future, we will make the plug-in compatible with a large number of video streaming websites. Furthermore, we will make it work on different platforms and streaming protocols (e.g. DASH, HLS), in order to capture the real user's experience of perceived video quality.

2.7.4. *Java application*

In parallel with the Firefox extension, we developed an application in JavaScript that runs as a background process for storing important information while a user is viewing an online video. This application has the main advantage of working on any video streaming website if it uses the TCP protocol as a transmission layer protocol. It monitors and collects all the information by periodically (5 seconds) checking the status of the terminal device and examining packet flow during video streaming. This application monitors real-time packets exchanged between the video server and the user while viewing the video stream. It extracts the required information by analyzing the packets without storing them, in order to compute the network performance statistics of QoS (packet loss, delay, jitter and throughput) during the video flow.

The application measures and stores different characteristics of the user's terminal device, e.g. CPU model specification, vendor name (e.g. Intel), speed and number of CPUs in the terminal device. Our framework tool carefully monitors the system's performance behavior in terms of memory and CPU usage while viewing the online video. It measures CPU usage (in percentage unit) during the video flow to determine the share of CPU power used in terms of the following parameters: user processes, system processes, idle, wait, nice, interrupt and combined usage (user+system). The application also measures the memory usage (in megabyte (MB)) to determine the amount of memory used by the system and how much is free. Initially, it stores all the information in the local database.

In future, we will add more functionalities in the framework to investigate the influence of more parameters on user-perceived quality. In the case of video streaming services, the following parameters could be monitored and stored in the local database: resolution, codec, content type, stalling time, user's buffering behavior in terms of the rebuffering event, minimum data required in the buffer before resuming the playback.

At the end of the crowdsourcing test, when all the parameters are extracted from the two modules (Java application and Firefox extension), the collected datasets are transferred from the user's terminal device to a distant server for investigating the user's QoE.

2.8. Conclusion

In this chapter, two different approaches were discussed to collect datasets for assessing the QoE of video services and analyze the impact of different parameters. The proposed approaches were the controlled and crowdsourcing environments. A testbed experiment was setup to measure the influence of different parameters on user-perceived QoE while watching the video service. The impact of different parameters (QoS parameters, video characteristic, device type, etc.) on user perception was recorded in the form of MOS.

The collected dataset was used to investigate the correlation between QoS and QoE. Six ML classification methods were used to classify the collected dataset. Among the classification methods, DT showed good performance with respect to the mean absolute error rate. An instance classification test was also performed to select the best model. The results showed that the performance of RF and DT was approximately at the same level. Finally, to evaluate the efficiency of DT and RF, a statistical analysis of the classification methods was carried out and the results showed that RF performed slightly better than DT.

The dataset allowed us to study the impact of different QoS parameters on users' profiles in order to achieve high user satisfaction of video streaming services. The comprehensive study of users' profiles from the perspective of QoS parameters gave useful information for network service providers to understand the behavior and expectations of end-users. The analysis showed that viewers of interesting video contents were more tolerant than those watching non-interesting video contents. Similarly, viewers of HD video contents were more sensitive to delay and packet loss rates, while they were more tolerant while watching non-HD video contents. Based on the analysis of users' profiles, network service providers can efficiently manage their resources to improve user satisfaction.

In the case of crowdsourcing, a new application tool was proposed to investigate users' QoE in the real-time environment. After the video playback, the tool took the user's feedback by automatically opening the feedback form. The user could also open and record the feedback to express his/her opinion of video quality by clicking the feedback button at the bottom of the display screen. The tool could monitor and store the performance of real-time QoS parameters (packet loss, delay, jitter and throughput). In addition to QoS networks, the tool also measured the real-time performance characteristics of the end-user's device in terms of system memory, performance capacity, CPU usage and other parameters.

This chapter dealt with the problem of assessing the QoE for video streaming by considering the influence of different parameters based on subjective datasets. Our collected dataset provided useful information about video quality, which is a crucial step towards developing an adaptive video streaming method that changes video quality based on network parameters and client device properties. In the following chapter, we will consider three influential QoS parameters (bandwidth, buffer, dropped frame rate) that significantly affect the user's QoE for HTTP-based video streaming. A client-side HTTP-based rate-adaptive method will be proposed to select the most suitable video quality based on the three QoS parameters.

3

Regulating QoE for Adaptive Video Streaming

In Chapter 2, we briefly discussed video streaming technologies over unmanaged networks, focusing mainly on Adobe's HDS adaptive video streaming technology. This chapter extends the investigation of the user's QoE from the perspective of three important parameters (bandwidth, buffer and dropped frame rate). It focuses on an adaptive method that can efficiently manage video streaming traffic according to different parameters in order to regulate the user's QoE.

3.1. Introduction

Video streaming is a main and growing contributor to Internet traffic. This growth results from deep changes in the technologies that are employed for delivering video content to end-users over the Internet. According to the Cisco forecast report, all forms of video (TV, Video on demand [VoD], Internet and P2P) will represent 80–90% of global consumer traffic by 2017 [CIS 13].

Traditionally, cable and IPTV services provide video services over a managed network as they use the multi-cast transport, where the required bandwidth is available for maximizing the user's Quality of Experience (QoE) (defined in [INT 07a]). However, in the age of multimedia technology, a large number of video-enabled electronic devices are made available, with the capacity to support a high-quality video playback. These devices include personal computers (PCs), laptop, smart phones, tablets, gaming consoles and

Internet-enabled televisions. In general, these devices access the video streaming services through unmanaged networks, e.g. local area network (LAN), WiFi hotspots and 3G/4G wireless networks.

Internet-based video, also known as Over-the-Top (OTT) services, can be divided into three different categories, such as user-generated content (e.g. DailyMotion, YouTube), professionally generated content (e.g. commercial), and movie sales to viewer over the Internet [BEG 11]. Content service providers ensure that video contents are available on the Internet in order to gain larger viewership. In general, video contents are delivered through a content delivery network (CDN), and different CDN architectures are used to improve the performance of the system, reduce network load and enhance the user-perceived QoE. In general, content is stored on the servers worldwide. The CDN algorithm tries to select servers that are close to the client in order to ensure a high-bandwidth video streaming. The most commonly used CDN providers include YouTube, Akamai, Netflix and Hulu. CDN providers use different mechanisms to select the suitable server to serve the end-user, because it is an important factor that influences the user-perceived quality of video services. In [ZHO 08b], the authors proposed a server selection method that selects the server based on the load information of replica servers, whereas the method proposed in [HAN 09] uses the minimum Round Trip Time (RTT) from the client in order to select the suitable server. In [TRA 14], the authors proposed a QoE-based server selection method that selects the appropriate server by considering the perceived QoE from each candidate server.

Furthermore, the demand of end-users to view the video contents at any time on any device over any access network brings new challenges to network operators and CDN providers to deliver the video content on different devices with maximum end-user QoE. Facing distinct network technologies and time-varying network conditions requires a video rate-adaptive method that considers not only network characteristics but also the properties of end-user's device to achieve high-quality video streaming. To overcome this problem, leading companies like Adobe, Microsoft, Apple and MPEG/3GPP have developed HTTP-based adaptive streaming technologies (see Chapter 2) that adapt video services to client and network properties. This adaptive method efficiently shares network resources (bandwidth) among the users and dynamically contributes to the network resource management with a high user-perceived QoE.

HTTP video streaming has the advantage of easily traversing NATs and firewalls unlike other media transport protocols such as RTP/RTSP. In HTTP adaptive streaming, the source video content (either a stored file or live stream) is broken into file segments, called fragments, chunks or segments, using the desired format, which contains video codec, audio codec, encryption protocol, etc. In general, the segment length is between 2 and 10 s of the stream. The segment file consists of either a multiplexing container that mixes the data from different tracks (video, audio, subtitles, etc.) or it can be a single track. The stream is divided into chunks at boundaries of video Group of Picture (GOP), identified by an IDR frame. The IDR frame can be decoded independently, without looking for other frames, and each chunk does not depend on previous and successive chunks. The file segments are hosted on a regular HTTP server (e.g. Apache server). The client adaptive player requests the appropriate video segment to the server, based on the network parameters and its machine-processing state.

Accurate bandwidth estimation is an important task, as it regulates the user's buffer and influences the user-perceived Quality of Service (QoS). In general, bandwidth is estimated using different pieces of information provided by the TCP protocol (e.g. Ack and RTT). In our proposed method, the video fragment size and download duration are used as the key parameters to estimate the client's bandwidth. The performance of rate-adaptive methods is significantly affected by the oscillation of the bandwidth. It is necessary to not only estimate the bandwidth but also handle an instantaneous fluctuation of bandwidth in an efficient way. The proposed method can estimate and manage the bandwidth fluctuation that regulates the user's buffer and copes with a sudden decrease in bandwidth.

In this chapter, a client-based rate-adaptive method BBF is proposed that dynamically selects the appropriate video quality based on network conditions and properties of the user's device. The network bandwidth significantly affects the video service, as it directly reduces the client buffering that may result in pausing or stalling during video streaming. The buffer length plays a vital role in reducing the influence of dynamic change in bandwidth. The proposed BBF method efficiently deals with sudden decrease in network bandwidth using new bandwidth metric and reduces its impact on the buffer level of the end-user. The dropped frame rate (fps) is another influential factor that has a negative impact on user's QoE. The BBF method considers three important QoS factors that regulate the user's QoE for video streaming over HTTP: Bandwidth, Buffer and dropped Frame rate (BBF). This chapter is based on our two IEEE conference papers[1,2].

3.2. Adaptive streaming architecture

HTTP-based adaptive streaming architecture mainly consists of three important components: client, delivery network and server.

Client-based adaptive HTTP streaming primarily depends on the adaptive method used by the client player. The main goal of adaptive streaming method is to dynamically select the appropriate video segment based on client device properties and network conditions. Figure 3.1 illustrates an adaptive streaming architecture that is based on a system model, which is described in section 3.6. In general, the main elements that regulate video streaming service at the client side are:

– player buffer, which stores the received video frames from the server;

– decoder, which decodes the received frames from the player buffer;

– buffer regulator, which controls the player buffer length in order to avoid buffer underflow/overflow condition;

– bandwidth estimator, which estimates the network bandwidth and requests the suitable segment to the server.

The client receives video frames in its player buffer that are later decoded to display the video stream to the user. The player buffer can contain different qualities of video frames, which influence the user-perceived QoE. The decoding process of video frames mainly depends on the available system resources of the user, because some video frames can be dropped due to insufficient local resources. In the case of recorded video streaming, especially when a video has high quality or high resolution, the decoder lags behind in decoding the required number of frames per second, because it does

1 M. Sajid Mushtaq, Brice Augustin, and Abdelhamid Mellouk. *Regulating QoE for Adaptive Video Streaming using BBF Method*. In Proc. of IEEE International Conference on Communications (ICC), London, UK, June 10-14, 2015.
2 M. Sajid Mushtaq, Brice Augustin, and Abdelhamid Mellouk. *HTTP Rata Adaptive Algorithm with High Bandwidth Utilization*. In Proc. of IFIP/IEEE International Conference on Network and Service Management (CNSM), Rio, Brazil, November 17-21, 2014.

not have enough system CPU resources that cause frame dropping. However, the player buffer can also drop the video frames when the latency is too high, particularly in live video streaming services. The user's QoE decreases when the number of dropped frames increases, as they are not presented to the user for viewing. In [ZIN 10], the authors used the full-reference model (compare received data with reference data) to study the impact of video frame rate and resolution on user's QoE.

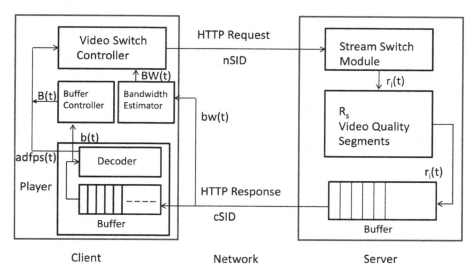

Figure 3.1. *Architecture of adaptive streaming*

To understand the dynamics of video playback buffer, it is necessary to consider the relationship between available network bandwidth and video rate in playback buffer, as shown in Figure 3.2, where the buffer size and buffer-filled length are measured in seconds. In [HUA 14c], the authors proposed a buffer-based adaptive method that uses the bandwidth and video rate relationship to avoid re-buffering. Let us consider if a 1 s video is removed from the buffer and playback, then the buffer is drained only for 1 s unit rate. However, when the player is paused, the buffer draining rate will be 0; in other words, the buffer draining rate $d(t)$ can be 0 or 1. In this chapter, the video segment duration is fixed at 4 s (i.e. 4 s per segment), and if the client requests a high video rate, then it requires larger segments (in bytes). When high video rate segment $R(t)$ is requested by the client and available bandwidth $B(t)$ is lower than the requested video rate, the buffer is filled at the rate $B(t)/R(t) < 1$, and as a result, the buffer decreases. If the client continuously requests high video quality at a rate greater than network bandwidth, the buffer might be depleted. As a result, playback will freeze and a re-buffering event will occur, thus decreasing the client's QoE. However, if network bandwidth is always higher than the requested video rate, then the client will never observe re-buffering events, i.e. $B(t)/R(t) > 1$.

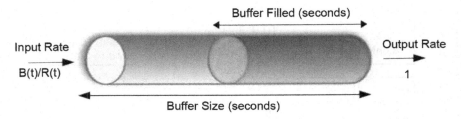

Figure 3.2. *Relationship between bandwidth B(t)*
and video rate R(t) in playback buffer

In adaptive streaming, the video is encoded into different bitrates. The player buffer length $q(t)$ [DEC 13, DEC 14a] can be modeled using the following expression:

$$q(t) = \frac{B(t)}{R(t)} - d(t) \qquad [3.1]$$

where $d(t)$ is the buffer draining rate, which can be modeled as follows:

$$d(t) = \begin{cases} 1 & \text{playing} \\ 0 & \text{paused} \end{cases} \qquad [3.2]$$

where $B(t)$ represents the received rate and $R(t)$ represents the received video level. The player buffer filling rate represents the number of seconds videos are stored in the buffer per second. The term $d(t)$ is the draining rate that represents the number of seconds of video played per second.

The video playback buffer directly depends on the video rate and available network bandwidth. From this perspective, it is mandatory that the main adaptive streaming controller at the client side consists of two sub-entities that regulate the video streaming service, i.e. buffer regulator and bandwidth estimator.

The buffer regulator tries to maintain the video buffer length within a certain bounded value. It primarily depends on the available network bandwidth: if the buffer draining rate is higher than the bandwidth, then the buffer will decrease, and an empty buffer event occurs, leading to the re-buffering stage. In [HUA 14b], a buffer-based rate adaptation method is proposed that selects and downloads the appropriate video segment, which is exclusively based on the client video buffer length and does not consider the available system capacity (bandwidth) at the client side. The bandwidth estimator measures the available network bandwidth at the client side. It determines the maximum client capacity to download the video stream rate. In general, the bandwidth estimator predicts the available bandwidth based on past transmission history. HTTP adaptive video streaming mostly uses TCP as a transport protocol, and the behavior of TCP during network congestion drastically influences the video quality. The adaptive streaming method should be robust to handle dynamic network conditions. The design of an adaptive streaming method consists of two steps: (1) selecting the appropriate video segment that matches the measured available bandwidth and (2) controlling the video playback buffer length using the idle time length between the downloading of two video segments. The general behavior of these two steps in adaptive video streaming can be observed in [DEC 14b, HUA 12, LI 14].

The delivery network can belong to a private organization that manages its own network for video services (e.g. video conference) or simply to an open public network (the Internet). The adaptive video streaming service uses the public Internet as its underlying delivery network, which is an unmanaged network. The Internet is a collection of diverse networks worldwide and it is constantly changing. The adaptive video streaming method considers the time-varying characteristics of the Internet to optimize the received video quality for improving the user-perceived QoE. In general, over the Internet, video streaming technologies send the video content from the server to the client using the standard delivery HTTP protocol over Transmission Control Protocol (TCP).

The server side contains a streaming switch mechanism module that selects the proper video quality based on the request received from the streaming switching controller at the client. The server contains different video segments, each of which has a specific playback duration, normally between 2 and 10 s. In the case of recorded video, the client first downloads a file that contains information about different video representations or profiles available at the server, i.e. manifest file. An XML-based manifest or SMIL [BUL 01] file contains information about the available video profiles. The client as a main controller has the full authority to regulate the video streaming and the server side follows the order from the client controller.

3.3. Video encoding

In adaptive video streaming, there are some critical elements in video encoding that should be taken into account for video quality stored at the server. The performance of an adaptive streaming method can be significantly affected when the important factors are not considered during the encoding process. The keyframe is a main contributing factor that affects the performance of adaptive streaming method. The BBF method uses the system implementation that is based on Adobe Flash platform, and videos are encoded using the H.264 codec, which contains three type of frames:

– I-frames: these are also known as keyframes, which are entirely self-referential without requiring data from other frames. From the viewpoint of compression, they are least efficient when compared with other frames (P and B).

– P-frames: these are "predicted" frames. The encoder produces a P-frame by considering only the previous I-frames or P-frames. They are more efficient than I-frames but less efficient than B-frames in terms of compression.

– B-frames: these are bidirectional predicted frames. When the encoder produces a B-frame, it considers both the forward and backward frames.

The video contents are encoded according to Adobe recommendation [ADO 10] using the Big Buck Bunny video file (YUV format). In the case of H.264 codec, the IDR and non-IDR I-frames are considered from different perspectives. Instantaneous Decoding Refresh (IDR) are common I-frames that guarantee a reliable seeking, because it allows succeeding frames reference itself and the frames after it, i.e. closed Group of Pictures (GOP). However, a non-IDR I-frame can be considered as an intra-coded P-frame, which is referenced by looking the preceding B-frames. The non-IDR

I-frames have the advantage that they improve the picture quality and smooth the P-to-I frame transition by reducing the I-frame flicker. The drawback of non-IDR I-frames is that the decoder has high start-up time as well as reducing the seeking precision.

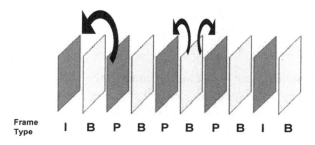

| Frame Type | I | B | P | B | P | B | P | B | I | B |

Figure 3.3. *H.264 frame*

The adaptive streaming method based on Flash platform only changes the video quality (bitrate) at IDR keyframe intervals (from here onward referred to as "keyframe"). The keyframe distance has vital impacts, e.g. seeking performance, decoder start-up time (in network streaming), recovery time from network errors and entire video quality. In general, keyframe distance is between 2 and 10 s. In the case of smaller distance (e.g. 2 s), the resulting video quality can change more quickly. The keyframe is larger than other frames (P and B frames), and it directly affects the video quality, as it follows the rule 2x rate. Let us consider a case when keyframe interval changes from 1 to 2 s, which will result in almost 2x the bitrate for quality improvement; when it changes from 2 to 3 s, it will give another 50% quality improvement and so on. The keyframe distance in frames can be calculated from equation [3.3], and results are formulated in Table 3.1.

Keyframe Distance = Frame Rate Frequency * Interval in seconds [3.3]

Table 3.1 illustrates the most-used frame rate frequencies in terms of different keyframe intervals. In the case of 60 Hz (60 fps), when the key frame interval increases from 1 to 2 s and keeps all other factors constant, the data rate is nearly doubled. Similarly, reducing keyframe interval by half (e.g. from 4 to 2 s) will reduce the video quality by half.

Frame Rate Frequency	Keyframe interval (in seconds)									
	1	2	3	4	5	6	7	8	9	10
60Hz (60fps)	60	120	180	240	300	360	420	480	540	600
30Hz (30fps)	30	60	90	120	150	180	210	240	270	300
25Hz (25fps)	25	50	75	100	125	150	175	200	225	250
24Hz (24fps)	24	48	72	96	120	144	168	192	216	240

Table 3.1. *Keyframe distance*

Smooth switching can be achieved among the different video qualities (bitrate) by keeping the same Sequence Parameter Set/Picture Parameter Set (SPS/PPS), Network Abstraction Level (NAL). Furthermore, the following important components should be considered:

– bitrate as a variable component among all possible switching bitrates;

– fixed frame size and same video duration across all switching bitrates;

– avoid scaling down from larger screens to smaller frames and vice versa.

3.4. Client–server communication

HTTP video streaming service is based on the communication between client and server with the TCP/IP protocols commonly used on the Internet for transmitting web pages from servers to the client. A web page is a collection of objects that are downloaded by using a persistent or non-persistent HTTP connection. In [TIA 12], the authors used a HTTP non-persistent connection, where each video segment is downloaded using a separate connection. In our proposed system implementation, we use a HTTP persistent connection. This shows high performance especially when video streaming shares available bandwidth with greedy TCP flows [DEC 13]. In addition, in [LED 12], the authors proved that a HTTP persistent connection shows a significant performance improvement over a non-persistent connection.

First, the client connects to the server via a web browser, and after successful connection, the flash application (player) is loaded in the browser in order to start the video streaming service. When the client starts the video streaming, a GET HTTP request is sent to the server. This initial request points out the manifest file (F4M) that is stored on the server and contains information about video meta data (e.g. video name, encoding video quality rate). After parsing the manifest file, the client player has complete information about the URL of each video quality level, and it can request the specific video quality level via a HTTP GET command, based on the decision made by its video stream switching controller.

Our proposed client player is based on Adobe streaming technology, where the server stores different video quality files for each available video. In Adobe technology, a video is logically segmented when compared with physically different segments of each video quality level, which are used by the Apply- and DASH-based HTTP adaptive streaming technologies. In Adobe adaptive streaming, the server stores each video quality level that is logically segmented (i.e. keyframe) but physically stored in a single file. Microsoft Smooth Streaming (MSS) technology uses the same technique. The main advantage of this technique is the reduced number of objects handled by the CDN.

The videos are encoded using the H.264 codec with Instantaneous Decoding Refresh (IDR) I-frames at 24 frames per second (fps). The stream is broken at Group of Pictures (GOP) boundaries that begin with IDR I-frames, and has length equal to 96, which means the distance between two I-frames (i.e. keyframes interval) is 4 s. The video quality level will change only at the IDR keyframe interval that can also have different profiles (e.g. resolution, 2D, etc.) for different devices.

When the client parses the manifest F4M file, it opens a TCP socket to send the HTTP GET request, pointing out specific video quality levels in the URL. The server sends the requested video quality level back to the client using the TCP protocol on the same socket, and this streaming procedure continues even during stream switching process using the same socket.

3.5. Rate-adaptive algorithm

A rate-adaptive algorithm is a method that changes the video quality based on network conditions, properties of end-user's device and other characteristics. In general, Internet video services run on unmanaged networks. Mostly, the video streaming technologies send the video content from the server to the client using the standard delivery HTTP protocol over TCP. HTTP has some advantages that enable universal access, availability of connection to many devices, reliability, mobile-fixed convergence, robustness and, last but not least, re-use of existing delivery infrastructure for larger distribution of media services. The main drawback of transport service over the HTTP protocol is the lack of bitrate guarantees. This deficiency of HTTP can be solved by enabling the client to dynamically select the appropriate video quality/bitrate segment of the same video content based on varying network conditions. Based on network conditions, TCP parameters provide vital information to the client, and streaming is managed by a rate-adaptive player at the client end.

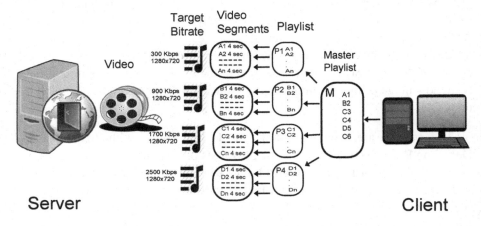

Figure 3.4. *Example: adaptive streaming*

Figure 3.4 illustrates a simple behavior of adaptive streaming under dynamic network conditions, and Figure 3.5 shows adaptive visual quality experience by the client. This example shows the rate-adaptive streaming, where only one video resolution is selected based on the display property of a client device, but it is encoded with distinct target bitrates in order to conform to client or network conditions. It is observable that a video with different target bitrates has the same segment duration, and it will help the client to easily switch the next video segment, either lower or higher video quality, based on the network condition. Each target video bitrate belongs to one playlist or profile, but the client gets the desired video segment from the different playlist, and makes its own playlist that is known as master playlist/profile. The master playlist contains different video segments based on the client device capabilities, network conditions, and preferences for optimal video quality experience as perceived by the end-user.

Figure 3.5. *Example: adaptive streaming sequence*

TCP parameters have a significant impact on the communication between the client and the server, especially in the transportation of adaptive video streaming. The analysis of TCP-based video streaming shows that TCP throughput should be double when compared with the video bitrate, which guarantees a smooth and good video streaming performance [WAN 08]. Adaptive video streaming tries to overcome this problem by adapting the video bitrate to the available network bandwidth. The network bandwidth has a direct influence on video quality selection, as the buffer is mainly affected by the network bandwidth. The buffer-based smooth adaptation method is discussed in [ZHO 13a], where the client-side buffer time is used as an important feedback parameter for avoiding buffer underflow/overflow.

3.6. System model

We consider x different video segments that are stored on the server. Each segment has a specific playback duration, and for simplicity, we assume that all segments have the same duration. In general, each segment has a duration between 2 and 10 s, and the proposed BBF method uses a segment length of 4 s. Each segment belongs to one video representation; in other words, one video is present in different sets of representations (different profiles). The available representations for a given video are denoted by R. The number of available representations in R represents the distinct aspects of a video. They might contain different video qualities encoded at different bitrates, different resolutions, or 2D or 3D video format. Normally, the recorded video representations are downloaded earlier by the client in the form of a manifest file, before it starts the playing session. An XML-based manifest (F4M) or SMIL [BUL 01] file contains the necessary information about the available video profiles.

Let us consider that the user requests the video from a streaming server. A set of suitable video representations for a specific user is denoted as R_s. If the user's device has a small screen with limited memory (e.g. smart phone), based on the user's device properties, a client-specific video representation should not include the high-resolution video, and similarly, it also does not take into account the high-quality video that consumes more memory. It is useless to send unsupported videos (e.g. of high resolution) to devices. In order to maximize user's QoE, an appropriate video representation should be selected based on device properties and network conditions.

In this study, a client player based on our proposed BBF method dynamically selects the appropriate video representation from R, and the client-specific video representation R_s contains a finite set of representation. A video representation r belongs to R_s ($R_s = r_1, r_2, ...r_n$), where r_1 denotes the lowest video quality and r_n denotes the high-quality video representation. We identify the current video stream by $cSID$ which denotes any r_i representation belonging to R_s. Similarly, the $nSID$ symbol denotes the next video stream identity that represents the r_{i+1} (possible higher quality) or r_{i-1} (possible lower quality) representation belonging to R_s. The adaptive method keeps monitoring the QoS parameters, because video quality switching is based on parameters related to video and network conditions.

The video playback starts immediately after completing the initial buffering requirement, i.e. there should be enough buffered video frame data in order to play back the video stream. We suppose that the video is buffered for $Period1$, as shown in Figure 3.6, and it starts playing. The video has j number of periods, and one period represents the playing duration of the video of the same quality. However, the adaptive player must make a decision about the video quality of the next period before the end of the current period. In the adaptive video streaming method, it is required that during the video playback period, available bandwidth, buffer and dropped video frames should be monitored continuously in order to adapt the video quality to time-varying parameters for the next period. Let us consider $Period1$ and $Period2$ as shown in Figure 3.6. To make sure that there will not be an interruption for video quality Rs (client-specific video) during the next playback time of $Period2$, we must simultaneously monitor the dynamic parameters (bandwidth, buffer and dropped video frame) at the client side. The playing duration of each period can be divided into n number of discrete time instants $(T_1, T_2, , T_n)$. It is not necessary that each playback Period has the same duration, e.g. in the case of aggressive buffer mode, the Period duration becomes half $(Period\ j/2)$ of normal Period, as it is essential to monitor the dynamic parameters more frequently to avoid a buffer empty state. The period length plays a significant role in estimating the QoS parameter (e.g. bandwidth) [THA 13]. The general expression for calculating the average buffer length B for the specific time period is given in equation [3.4]:

$$B_j = \frac{\sum_{i=1}^{n_j} b_{i,j}}{(n_j)}, n_j = 1, 2, ...n \qquad [3.4]$$

where $b_{i,j}$ is the measurement of instantaneous buffer for $Period\ j$ at time instance i. Let us consider the case for the next playback $Period2$; the instance buffer $b_{1,1}$ is calculated at time T_{11} for $Period1$; similarly, next instance buffer $b_{2,1}$ represents the time T_{21} and so on. In the BBF method, we set the instantaneous time to 150 ms. The general expression to calculate the dropped frame is given in equation [3.5]:

$$dfps = \frac{(df - pdfps)}{ct - tpdfps} \qquad [3.5]$$

where df is the number of video frames dropped in the current video playback session and $pdfps$ is the number of video frames dropped in the previous playback session. The current time is denoted by ct, whereas $tpdfps$ represents the time when $pdfps$ occurred. In recorded video streaming, when a downloaded video has a high quality or high resolution, the client might drop frames df because of insufficient system CPU resources to decode the required number of frames per second. In live streaming, the buffer drops video frames if the latency is too high. This property df specifies the number of frames that were dropped and not presented to the user for viewing. First, the dropped frame rate can be valid only if there are enough downloaded video data. In our case, the average dropped video frame rate ($adfps$) can be calculated from equation [3.6] as follows:

$$adpfs_j = \frac{\sum_{i=1}^{n_j} dfps_{i,j}}{(n_j)}, n_j = 1, 2, ...n \qquad [3.6]$$

where $dfps$ represents the video dropped frame per second. Similarly, the average bandwidth (BW) is calculated from equation [3.7] as follows:

$$BW_j = \frac{\sum_{i=1}^{n_j} bw_{i,j}}{(n_j)}, n_j = 1, 2, ...n \qquad [3.7]$$

where $bw_{i,j}$ is the measurement of instantaneous bandwidth for $Period\ j$ at time instance i, as explained earlier in the case of buffer. The instantaneous bandwidth value bw is calculated by dividing the downloaded fragment size and download duration of that fragment. The weighting vector is used to calculate the bandwidth on the recent sample plus last downloaded sample. The BBF method uses the weighting vector $[7, 3]$ by considering the two fragments, where higher weight is assigned to the recent fragment sample. By exponentially averaging the bandwidth BW_j, the maximum bandwidth can be calculated using equation [3.8]:

$$BW_{max(j)} = (\theta)BW_{max(j-1)} + (1 - \theta)\frac{BW_j + BW_{j-1}}{2} \qquad [3.8]$$

The estimated maximum bandwidth (BW_{max}) is used to regulate the client's buffer. The parameter θ is a weighting factor that finds out the last two bandwidth sample weights against the history of estimated bandwidth. We conducted experiments with different θ values and observed that the proposed BBF algorithm performs well when θ value is close to 1. The BBF method uses $\theta = 0.8$.

3.7. Proposed BBF method

The pseudo-code of our proposed BBF rate-adaptive algorithm is presented in two sub-algorithms for simplicity and better understanding, but we refer them as a single algorithm. Algorithm 4.1 deals with a case when certain conditions are fulfilled to switch down the current video quality, whereas Algorithm 4.2 considers a case when the video is switched up on a higher quality based on the maximum bandwidth. The BBF algorithm dynamically selects an appropriate set of video representations R_s based on the user's device properties (e.g. screen resolution). In order to minimize the initial playback time, the algorithm selects the lowest video quality. It starts playing the video as soon as the initial segments are downloaded, and the buffer length (in seconds) reaches the start buffer length B_s. In the case of quick start, B_s must be set to a low value, but it is necessary to set its value to be high enough, so it will be easy to compute the maximum bandwidth available for the stream. When a stream begins to play, the algorithm considers the preferred buffer length B_p, instead of B_s. B_p is the length of buffer (in seconds), after a stream begins playing. The value of B_p should be higher than B_s. The value of B_p represents the preferable buffer length, and it does not illustrate the current buffer length B while playing the video streaming.

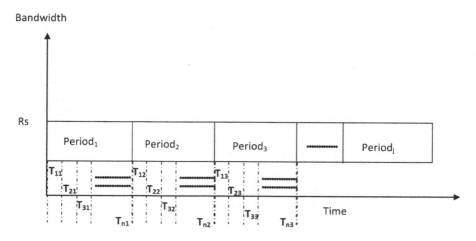

Figure 3.6. *Time vs. bandwidth*

The maximum bandwidth capacity available for video stream is represented by BW_{max}, which is calculated from equation [3.7]. It represents a client bandwidth, not a server bandwidth, and its value changes according to network conditions to which the client is currently exposed. The currently playing video stream is identified by $cSID$ which denotes any r_i (*i.e.* $i = 1, 2, \ldots. n$) representation belonging to R_s; similarly, the symbol

$nSID$ denotes the possible next video stream identity that represents the r_{i+1} (possible high quality) or r_{i-1} (possible low quality) representation belonging to R_s.

The BBF algorithm also monitors the video stream in terms of the number of frames per second (fps). In such a circumstance, when an average video dropped frame per second ($adfps$) is higher (more than 10%), it becomes necessary to make a decision in order to adopt lower video quality, as it influences the user-perceived video quality. In [ZIN 10], the authors studied the impact of video frame rate and resolution on QoE using the full-reference measurement method.

Two more buffers are considered in the BBF algorithm: current buffer time B_c and buffer time B_t. Initially, B_c is equal to B_s, but later it contains the same value as B_p and at the end of video streaming, B_c will be empty. On the contrary, B_t specifies how long to buffer a video before starting to display the stream. In order to avoid distortion when streaming a pre-recorded (not live) video content, the rate-adaptive video player uses an input buffer (here B_c) for the pre-recorded content that queues the media data and plays the media properly. The BBF algorithm also takes into account the worst-case scenario when the buffer is in underflow condition. In order to avoid buffer underflow condition that causes video streaming interruption in form of stalling or pausing, an aggressive buffer length B_a is introduced. If the user buffer length B is less than B_a, then a video stream switches to the lowest possible bitrate in order to avoid the buffer from emptying, because an empty buffer can cause a pause or stutter in video streaming. However, by shifting to a lower possible video quality, it is necessary to check the QoS parameters more frequently to maximize the user's QoE.

Table 3.2 contains information about all symbols or abbreviations used in the BBF algorithm. The proposed BBF algorithm considers three main parameters, B, BW_{max} and $adfps$, in order to switch to lower or higher video quality. However, when the conditions for switching down to lower video bitrate are not fulfilled (i.e. Algorithm 3.1), the algorithm considers the other condition to shift up the video bitrate (i.e. Algorithm 3.2). The BBF algorithm adapts video streaming by taking into account the following conditions:

Words	Abbreviations
Next Stream ID	nSID
Current Stream ID	cSID
Average Maximum Bandwidth	BW_{max}
Client Specific Video Representation	R_s
Average Buffer Length	B
Start Buffer Length	B_s
Preferred Buffer Length	B_p
Aggressive Buffer Length	B_a
Current Buffer Time	B_c
Current Stream Bitrate	cSBR
Buffer Time	B_t
Current Time	c_t
Current Frame Per Second	fps
Dropped Frame	df
Average Dropped Frame Per Second	adfps
Dropped Frame Per Second	dfps
Previous Dropped Frame Per Second	pdfps
Time Previous Dropped Frame	tpdfps

Table 3.2. *List of abbreviations used in the algorithm*

Algorithm 3.1.

Rate Adaptive Algorithm Switch Down

Input: A finite set $R_s = \{r_1, r_2, \ldots, r_n\}$ of client specific video

Output: Select appropriate video $(nSID)$ for end user

Result: Video quality switched down

Conditions to switch down video quality

if ($B < B_p$ **or** $BW_{max} < cSBR$ **or** (fps>0 *and* adfps>0.10))

{

 if ($B < B_p$ **or** $BW_{max} < cSBR$)

 {

  $i \leftarrow$ length of R_s

  {

   if ($BW_{max} > R_s(i)$)

    { $nSID \leftarrow i; break$ }

   $i \leftarrow i - 1$

  }

while $i \geq 0$
if ($nSID < cSID$)
  {
if ($BW_{max} < cSBR$)
{ Switch down due to less bandwidth }
else
{
if ($B < B_c$)
    { Switch down due to buffer }
      }
  }
if ($B > B_c$ **and** $B_c! = B_p$)
{
$B_c \leftarrow B_p$
$B_t \leftarrow B_c$
}
}
else
{
Switching down as adfps is greater than 10%
if ($adfps >= 10\%$ and $adfps < 14\%$)
{ $nSID \leftarrow cSID - 1$ }
if ($adfps >= 14\%$ and $adfps <= 20\%$)
{ $nSID \leftarrow cSID - 2$ }
if ($adfps > 20\%$)
{ $nSID \leftarrow 0$ }
}
if ($B < B_a$)
{
Switch down to lowest quality to avoid interruption $nSID \leftarrow 0$
    check QoS more frequently
}   }
else
{
Switch Up on Maximum Bandwidth
Run Algorithm 4 "Rate Adaptive Algorithm Switch up"
}

Algorithm 3.2.

Rate Adaptive Algorithm Switch Up

Input: A finite set $R_s = \{r_1, r_2, \ldots, r_n\}$ of client specific video

Output: Select appropriate video $(nSID)$ for end user

Result: Video quality switched up

Conditions to Switch Up video quality

If $(B < B_p$ **or** $BW_{max} < cSBR$ **or** (fps>0 and adfps>0.10))

Run Algorithm 3.1. "Rate Adaptive Algorithm Switch down"

else

{

Switch Up on Maximum Bandwidth

$nSID \leftarrow 0$

$i \leftarrow$ length of R_s

while $i \geq 0$

   {

       if $(BW_{max} > R_s(i))$

       $\{ nSID \leftarrow i; break \}$ $i \leftarrow i - 1$

}   if $(nSID < cSID)$

$\{ nSID \leftarrow cSID \}$

else

{

if $(nSID > cSID)$

{

switch-up only if find good buffer level   if $B < B_c$

$\{ nSID \leftarrow cSID \}$

    }

   }

}

Switch down to a lower video bitrate

– When the available maximum bandwidth BW_{max} is lower than the current video stream bitrate $cSRB$.

– When the client buffer length B is less than current buffer time B_c.

– When dropped frame per second $adfps$ is greater than 10%.

– In aggressive mode, when the client buffer length B is less than the aggressive buffer length B_a.

Switch up to a high video bitrate

– When the available maximum bandwidth BW_{max} is higher than the current video stream bitrate $cSBR$, but only if we find a good buffer level (i.e. $B > B_c$).

3.8. Experimental setup

The experiential setup contains three important elements: a video streaming server, a video-enabled client machine and a network emulator. The network emulator tools are used to emulate the real-time networks, and two most-used tools are DummyNet [CAR 10b] and built-in linux NetEm [LIN 16]. We use the NetEm as a network emulator to evaluate the proposed BBF algorithm. The experimental setup is shown in Figure 3.7, where traffic flows between the client and the server via network emulator. The client sends the video request message via a HTTP GET command to the video server by using the IP networks (LAN), and in response, the requested video is sent to the client. The server stores multiple copies of a single video, but in different video qualities (bitrates). The video content "Big Buck Bunny" is stored on the Apache streaming server, and it has a duration of almost 10 min that is suitable for evaluating the BBF method. The server contains the video contents that are encoded at 10 different video bitrates, as given in Table 3.3. When $adfps \geq 20\%$, the BBF method locks the video quality for 15 s in order to avoid quality decline again.

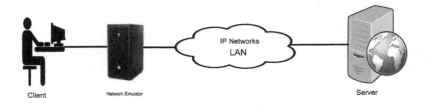

Figure 3.7. *Experimental setup*

3.9. Results

The BBF rate-adaptive method is evaluated in a controlled environment in the form of a testbed, where the available network bandwidth and user buffer fluctuate. Their impact on user-perceived quality is observed while watching the video streaming. The evaluation is done using the wired Local Area Network (LAN), where the network emulator (NetEm) [LIN 16] tool is used to control the network bandwidth between the client and the server. First, the BBF-based player is evaluated in terms of different buffer lengths, which illustrates the importance of different buffer lengths in selecting the suitable video quality under dynamic network conditions. The evaluation condition is the same for all cases, and three buffer lengths (60, 30 and 15 s) are provided. Later, the proposed method is compared to Adobe's OSMF streaming method.

Videos	Bitrate (kbps)
1	300
2	600
3	900
4	1,200
5	1,700
6	2,100
7	2,500
8	3,000
9	3,500
10	4,000

Table 3.3. *Video content quality*

Figure 3.8 shows the behavior of the client's player in terms of bandwidth, buffer and dropped frame rate, when the buffer length is set to 60 s. First, the BBF player starts buffering and playing the lowest video quality to reduce the start-up delay. In the meantime, it estimates the available bandwidth and starts buffering the next possible video quality. The frame rate behavior that influences the selection of video quality is shown in Figure 3.8(a) and Figure 3.8(b) depicts the buffer length. When dropped frame rate exceeds 10% (at t=174 s), and when the buffer length is shorter than 60 s (at 270, 340, 488, 540 s), video stream is shifted down to lower quality. The player performance is evaluated when the bandwidth is reduced to 2,000 kbps (2 Mbps) at 250 s, which is half of maximum video quality (4,000 kbps). The dropping-off bandwidth also drags down the buffer level, which causes the video to shift to lower quality (at 270 s) in order to avoid jerking or pausing in video streaming. In addition, the drop in bandwidth also forces the video to switch down to lower video bitrate (at 300 s) The bandwidth increases again to 5,000 kbps (higher than maximum video quality) at 350 s, and the client player successfully shifts up to the suitable video quality by considering the bandwidth and buffer level.

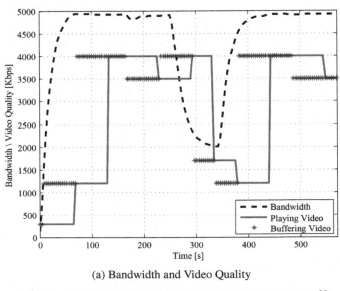

(a) Bandwidth and Video Quality

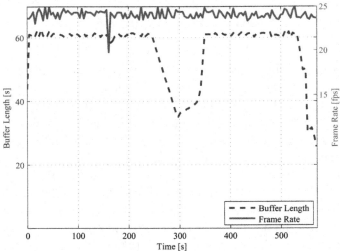

(b) Buffer Length and Frame Rate

Figure 3.8. *Client video adaptive streaming when the buffer length is 60 s*

Figure 3.9 shows the result of the BBF method when the buffer length is 30 s, and it considers three QoS factors (bandwidth, buffer and dropped frame rate) in order to select the suitable video quality index. First, the player starts streaming the lowest video quality (300 kbps), then switches to 2,100 kbps and later to 4,000 kbps in an aggressive way based on the bandwidth and buffer. It switches again to lowest video quality "300 kbps"' (at 113 s), when the dropped frame rate is 21%, as shown in Figure 3.9(b). In the case of a sudden decrease in network bandwidth, forces decrease the buffer level, which causes the video to switch down to next lower video quality based on the bandwidth and the buffer length. When the bandwidth reaches 2,000 kbps, video quality shifts are totally based on the buffer length. Later, the bandwidth increases again to 5,000 kbps (at 350 s), and afterward video quality switches up to the highest quality index (4,000 kbps).

Figure 3.10 represents the performance of the BBF rate-adaptive method, when the buffer length is set to 15 s. The two sharp drops in video quality (from 4,000 to 300 kbps) occur due to high dropped frame rate (more than 20%) at 220 and 468 s. When the lock timer (15 s) expires, the video switches again to the highest possible level by considering the bandwidth and buffer level. The impact of sudden decreases in bandwidth starts at 265 s, which causes the reduction in video quality. When bandwidth reaches 2,000 kbps, video switch down occurs because of the buffer length. The bandwidth increases again to more than 4,000 kbps, which results in a switch up of video quality in an aggressive way by considering the available bandwidth.

It is observed that a greater buffer length is less affected by the time-varying properties of the network, but it does not efficiently use network resources and reduces user's QoE.

The performance of the BBF method is compared to that of the Adobe OSMF adaptive streaming method. The evaluation is based on the behavior of adaptive streaming method during the sudden decrease in bandwidth and dropped frame rate. The network bandwidth is reduced to half of the maximum available video bitrate when the video of highest quality is playing, and the ability of an adaptive method to manage this scenario is observed. Similarly, the effects of buffer level and dropped frame rate are observed on both adaptive methods.

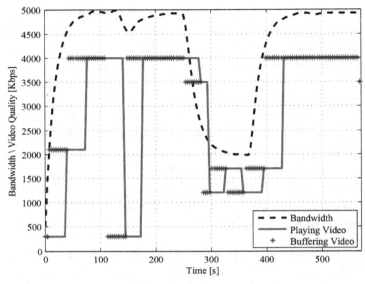

(a) Bandwidth and Video Quality

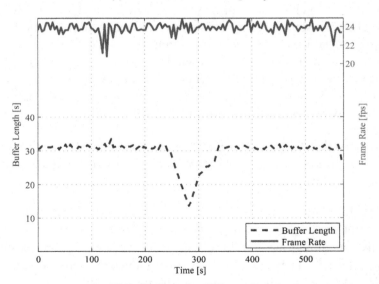

(b) Buffer Length and Frame Rate

Figure 3.9. *Client video adaptive streaming*
when the buffer length is 30 s

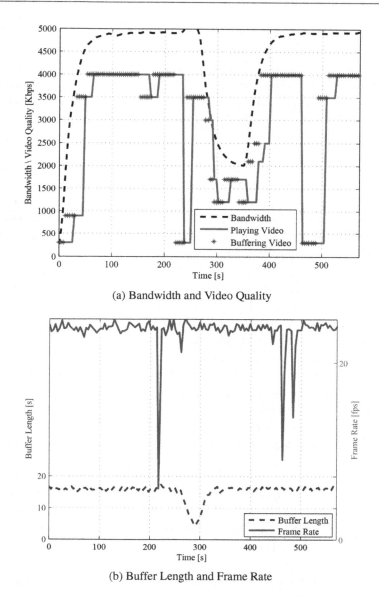

(a) Bandwidth and Video Quality

(b) Buffer Length and Frame Rate

Figure 3.10. *Client video adaptive when the buffer length is 15 s*

Figure 3.11 shows the performance of BBF method, and Figure 3.12 represents the operation of Adobe's OSMF player in terms of bandwidth, buffer and dropped fame rate. First, the BBF method starts playing a video of the lowest quality (300 kbps); meanwhile, based on the current bandwidth and the buffer length, it starts buffering the next possible video stream index, as illustrated in Figure 3.11(a). When the buffer level is equal to or greater than 15 s, the BBF method increases the video quality based on the available bandwidth. The video quality increases purely based on the bandwidth in an aggressive way, compared with the step-by-step manner in OSMF, as shown in Figure 3.12(a).

When $adfps \geq 10\%$, the BBF method switches down by one video quality level, but it switches down two quality levels if $14\% \leq adfps < 20\%$. In other cases, it switches down to lower video quality (e.g. 300 kbps) when $adfps \geq 20\%$. In Figure 3.11(a) the decrease in video quality to 300 kbps at 109 s occurs due to dropping of frame rate by more than 40%, and the BBF method locks the video quality (4,000 kbps) for few seconds (15 s) in order to avoid switching again to a lower video quality. Later, we observe that the video quality switches up to 3,500 kbps instead of 4,000 kbps, as the available bandwidth is higher than the high-quality video, but the current buffer length does not allow any change in the high-quality video at 130 s, as shown in Figure 3.11. In Figure 3.12, it is observed that the OSMF player switches down two quality levels (3,000 kbps), but suddenly moves up to the next level (3,500 kbps), as it has a small buffer length (5 s), and it locks the video quality index for 2 min, which causes the decrease in video quality. The small buffer length can react quickly to changes in network condition, but a sudden decrease in bandwidth may cause the buffer to flash empty, which leads to pausing, stalling and jerking in video streaming, which reduces user's QoE.

We reduce the available bandwidth to 2,000 kbps to observe the response of BBF and OSMF player. We observe that the BBF method successfully manages to handle the decrease in bandwidth. It switches down the video quality step by step according to the bandwidth and buffer level. The bandwidth forces the buffer level to decrease quickly, as shown in Figure 3.11(b) at 255 s. The BBF method supervises the situation, and based on the buffer length (less than 4 s), it aggressively shifts the video quality to the lowest level to avoid the pausing, jerking and stalling in video streaming. On the contrary, the OSMF player is unable to handle the sudden decrease in bandwidth, as its buffer flashes empty. This also causes high dropped frame rate, which blocks the video quality from switching up for 2 min despite high bandwidth. The user observes the pausing, stalling and jerking in video streaming, which significantly minimizes user's QoE. In the case of OSMF, we note that when the video quality locks for a longer period, it does not efficiently utilize the bandwidth, as shown in Figure 3.12(a), during 300–400 s.

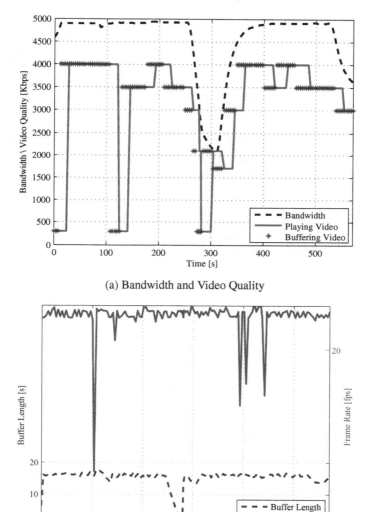

(a) Bandwidth and Video Quality

(b) Buffer Length and Frame Rate

Figure 3.11. *BBF video adaptive method*

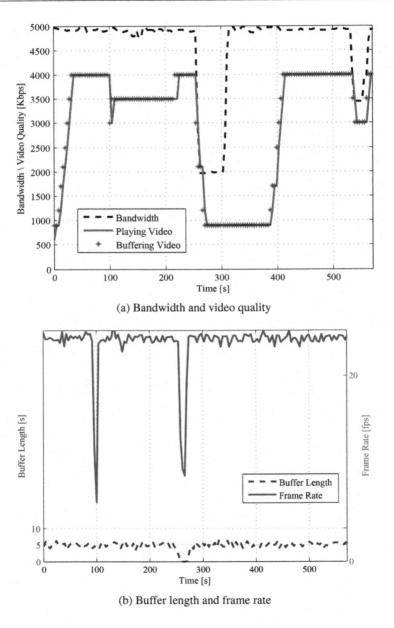

(a) Bandwidth and video quality

(b) Buffer length and frame rate

Figure 3.12. *OSMF video adaptive method*

In Figure 3.11(a), the video switches down by one quality level (at 397 and 446 s) due to a drop of 10% frame rate, and the last decline in video quality occurs due to buffer level at 543 s. In the case of OSMF, Figure 3.12(a) shows that the video quality changes only when the bandwidth decreases at 530 s, with no decrease in the buffer level and frame rate as shown in Figure 3.12(b).

3.10. Conclusion

In this chapter, we discussed HTTP rate-adaptive video streaming services over the TCP protocol. We pointed out the role of several components in an adaptive video streaming architecture. Video encoding is an essential step that influences the performance of the whole adaptive streaming system. The key elements in video encoding were presented, and their impact on the adaptive video streaming service was highlighted. The basic client–server communication in an adaptive video streaming system was described, in which the client downloaded the manifest file to know the available different video representations on the server. The client only requested the appropriate video representation according to the available network and device characteristics. The working behavior of the rate-adaptive method was presented, and we showed that the client made its own playlist of different video qualities based on network properties and device status.

The BBF method was proposed to consider the three main QoS parameters in order to adapt the video quality. The system model used by the proposed BBF method was presented. The system model described the working behavior of the BBF method, and how it computed the different metrics used in selecting the suitable video quality. The proposed client-side rate-adaptive BBF method adapted the video quality based on the dynamic network bandwidth, user's buffer status and dropped frame rate. The BBF method was evaluated with different buffer lengths, and the result showed that a greater buffer length was less affected by dynamic bandwidth, but the network resources were also not efficiently utilized. The BBF method was evaluated and compared with Adobe's OSMF streaming method. The results showed that the BBF method successfully managed situations when compared with OSMF, in terms of sudden decreases in bandwidth and drops in frame rate when the client system did not have enough resources to decode the frames. In addition, the BBF method optimized the user's QoE by avoiding stalling and pausing during video playback.

Chapter 4 will describe the methods used to measure the user-perceived QoE for VoIP multimedia traffic. We will propose a new downlink scheduling algorithm for Long-Term Evolution-Advanced (LTE-A) networks to allocate radio resources to the end-user by measuring the in-speech user's QoE and other parameters of VoIP traffic.

QoE-based Power Efficient
LTE Downlink Scheduler

In Chapter 3, we discussed the role of different parameters in regulating the user's QoE of HTTP-based adaptive video streaming services. The proposed adaptive BBF method considered the QoS parameters to adapt the video quality. The communication world moves toward an all-IP trend, where all services will be based on IP together with essential features and functions. The current Fourth-Generation (4G) wireless Long-Term Evolution-Advanced (LTE-A) system and future 5G networks will also follow the same all-IP trends. Despite ever-increasing video traffic in the IP world, VoIP is still considered as the main revenue stream for future wireless communication networks. Powerful mobile devices have capabilities to support VoIP service in wireless networks. It is difficult to measure subjectively user's QoE for in-service speech quality. The 4G standard of LTE-A wireless system has adopted the discontinuous reception (DRX) method to extend and optimize the UE battery life, while there is no standard scheduling method to distribute the radio resources among the UE. This chapter presents a downlink scheduler, i.e. Quality of Experience (QoE) power efficient method (QEPEM) for LTE-A, which efficiently allocates the radio resources and optimizes the use of UE power through the DRX mechanism. The QEPEM uses the E-Model to measure the user's QoE for in-speech VoIP multimedia traffic at the user side. Later, each user provides feedback of its perceived quality to the evolving NodeB (eNodeB), where the QEPEM downlink scheduler for the LTE-A network decides to allocate the radio resources to the end-user based on distinct parameters (e.g. DRX status and channel quality). This chapter also investigates how the different duration of DRX Light and Deep Sleep cycles influence the QoS and QoE of end-users, using VoIP over the LTE-A. The QEPEM is evaluated with the traditional methods, in terms of System Throughput, Fairness Index, Packet Loss Rate and Packet Delay. Our proposed QEPEM reduces packet delay and packet loss and increases fairness and UE's power saving with high user satisfaction. This chapter is based on our two journal articles[1,2].

4.1. Introduction

The tremendous growth in consumer electronic devices with enhanced capabilities, together with the improved capacities of wireless networks, has led to a vast growth in multimedia services. The new trends in the electronic market have led to the development of various smart mobile devices (e.g. iPhone, iPad and Android), which are powerful enough to support a wide range of multimedia applications. Meanwhile, there is an increasing demand for high-speed data services; 3rd Generation Partnership Project (3GPP) introduced the modern radio access technology, LTE and LTE-Advanced (henceforth referred to as LTE). The LTE has the ability to provide larger bandwidth and low latencies on a wireless network in order to fulfill the demand of UEs with acceptable QoS, and works on future mobile systems (5G) to provide more freedom in terms of capacity and connectivity, supporting the diverse set of services, applications and UEs together with efficient power utilization. In line with advanced network technology, a large number of data applications are also developed for smart mobile devices, which motivates users to access the LTE network more frequently [ETS 11a].

Initially, 3GPP improves the LTE wireless system by means of important performance parameters such as high capacity and lower latencies and by offering emerging multimedia service (e.g. VoIP, HD video streaming, multi-player interactive gaming and real-time video). It is necessary to

---

1 M. Sajid Mushtaq, Abdelhamid Mellouk, Brice Augustin, and Scott Fowler, "QoE Power-Efficient Multimedia Delivery Method for LTE-A", *IEEE System Journal*, 2015.
2 M. Sajid Mushtaq, Scott Fowler, Abdelhamid Mellouk, and Brice Augustin, "QoE/QoS-aware LTE downlink scheduler for VoIP with power saving", *Elsevier International Journal of Networks and Computer Applications (JNCA)*, 2015.

manage these performance parameters in an efficient manner. A key performance parameter on the UE electronics device is power because emerging multimedia services require computationally complex circuitry that drains the UE battery power quickly, as data transmission bandwidth is limited by the battery capacity [ETS 12].

Voice over IP (VoIP) is a commonly used low-cost service for voice calls over IP networks. The success of VoIP is mainly influenced by user satisfaction, in the context of quality of calls when compared with conventional fixed telephone services. Initially, the implementation of VoIP services was unable to tackle the unpredictable behavior of IP networks, which significantly affected the growth of early VoIP services, because its traffic streams are both slow and less sensitive. It is a main challenge for VoIP services to provide the same QoS as a conventional telephone network, i.e. reliable and with a QoS guarantee.

The bearer quality is managed as a single quality plan in conventional networks, while in next-generation networks (NGNs), it is also necessary to manage the end-user's QoE. In a wireless system, the unpredictable air interface behaves differently for each UE. In these circumstances, it is necessary to monitor the QoE in the network on a call-by-call basis [ETS 02].

The main challenge in any wireless system is to optimize the power consumption at the UE. The DRX method is not a novel approach in LTE [ETS 11b] because the existing cellular communication systems (e.g. GSM and UMTS) use it to optimize power consumption at the UE. In the Universal Mobile Telecommunications System (UMTS), the DRX method uses two cycles: Inactivity for UE wakeup and DRX cycle for sleep. The main difference between LTE and the early DRX method is that the UE can switch to the sleep state even if the traffic buffer is not empty [FOW 12]. In LTE, the DRX states (e.g. Inactivity) depend on scheduling because it increases the UE's active time by re-initializing the Inactive cycle. The idea is to optimize the UE's battery life, so that it does not run out of power too quickly.

To save the power of UE, the LTE specification uses the DRX method together with Light Sleep and Deep Sleep methods. In the DRX Light Sleep method, the UE enters into sleep mode for a shorter period of time. The UE consumes less power in this method than in normal active operational mode because UE does not switch off its receiver completely. Meanwhile, the UE's receiver switches between active and sleep modes periodically to receive the scheduled packets. In certain cases, when the UE does not receive the packet for a long period, the UE goes into the DRX Deep Sleep mode and turns off its receiver completely. The DRX Deep Sleep mode has a longer duration than the DRX Light Sleep mode and does not consume any power. The multimedia traffic is directly influenced by DRX Sleep mode because increased power saving will result in more packet delays or packet loss. Thus it is required to optimize the DRX parameters for maximum power saving without degrading network performance that directly influences the service quality experienced by the user, especially for real-time multimedia services (e.g. VoIP and video streaming). In this context, our proposed scheduling method plays an important role that considers the DRX parameters in its scheduling decision for best network performance and maximum user QoE.

Many network researchers are now working on this concept and trying to integrate it in network decisions to ensure a high customer satisfaction with minimum network resources. The proposed QEPEM algorithm makes the scheduling decision by considering the user satisfaction factor. In general, QoE is considered as a subjective measure of user satisfaction of a given service. According to [INT 07a], the standard definition of QoE is: a measure of the overall acceptability of an application or service, as perceived subjectively by the end-user.

As we have discussed in Chapter 2, there are two methods to evaluate the quality of multimedia services: the subjective method and the objective method. The subjective method is proposed by the International Telecommunication Union (ITU-T) Rec. P.800 [INT 96], which is mostly used to determine the user perception of the quality of speech. The mean opinion score (MOS) is an example of a subjective measurement method, in which users rate the voice quality by giving five different point scores, from 5 to 1, where 5 is the best quality and 1 is the worst quality. On the contrary, the objective method uses different models of human expectations and tries to estimate the performance of speech service in an automated manner, without human intervention. It is very difficult to measure subjectively the MOS of in-service speech quality because the MOS is a numerical average value of a large number of user opinions. Therefore, objective speech quality measurement methods are developed to make a good estimation of MOS. The

E-model [INT 11] and perception evaluation of speech quality (PESQ) [INT 01a] are objective methods for measuring the MOSs. PESQ cannot be used to monitor the QoE for real-time calls because it uses a reference signal and compares it to the real-time degraded signal for calculating the MOS. Therefore, we have used the E-model computational method to calculate the MOS of conversation quality by the latency (delay) and packet loss rate using the transmission rating factor (R-factor) [INT 11].

In this chapter, we propose a downlink scheduling method, called the QEPEM, for LTE networks that uses an opportunistic approach to calculate the priorities of UEs based on user perception (QoE), and other important parameters for assigning the radio resources among UEs. The main objective is to enhance the user satisfaction by monitoring the MOS of each UE. The priorities of UEs are calculated by considering the following parameters: MOS, channel condition, average throughput, UE buffer status, UE DRX status and guaranteed bitrate (GBR) or non-GBR traffic. The performance of the QoE scheme is compared with that of two traditional scheduling schemes: Proportional Fair (PF) and Best Channel Quality Indicator (BCQI). Two traditional methods are selected because they perform well in some QoS metrics according to the network conditions, and these are discussed later. The performance assessment is carried out for loss- and delay-sensitive VoIP multimedia traffic, and its impact on QoE is evaluated using an LTE system-level simulator.

4.2. An overview of LTE

To meet the increasing demand of high-speed data services, such as conversational voice, video and online gaming, the 3GPP introduced the new radio access technology, LTE. The radio network architecture proposed by the 3GPP LTE consists of evolved NodeB (eNodeB), which provides a link between UE and core network. The eNodeB is responsible for the major radio resource management (RRM) functions, such as packet scheduling. The UE is connected with eNodeB via the Uu interface. The eNodeB is connected to core network (MME/S-GW) via the S1 interface, and each eNodeB is inter-connected via the X2 interface, as shown in Figure 4.1. The Mobility Management Entity (MME) is an important part of the LTE architecture, which is responsible for paging and UE mobility in idle mode within the network. The Serving Gateway (S-GW) node is responsible for routing user data packets and handling other user requests, e.g. handover. The MME and S-GW are part of the core network.

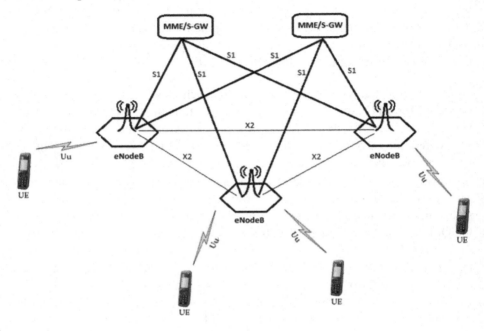

Figure 4.1. *LTE architecture*

LTE uses orthogonal frequency division multiple access (OFDMA) as a radio interface, which divides the bandwidth into sub-carriers and assigns them to the users depending on their current demand of service. Each sub-carrier carries data at low rates, but at the same time uses multiple sub-carriers to provide high data rates [RAM 09].

There are some advantages of OFDM when compared with other techniques. First, OFDM uses multiple-carrier transmission techniques, which makes the symbol time substantially larger than channel delay spread. Consequently, the effect of intersymbol interference (ISI) reduces significantly. In other words, against the multi-path interference (frequency-selective fading), OFDM provides high robustness with less complexity. Second, using fast Fourier transform (FFT) processing, OFDM allows low-complexity implementation. Third, OFDM offers complete freedom to the scheduler using the frequency access technique (OFDMA). Finally, it provides spectrum flexibility, which helps to achieve smooth evolution from all the existing radio access technologies toward LTE.

Each downlink frame in LTE lasts 10 ms and contains 10 sub-frames. Each sub-frame has a duration of 1 ms, which is known as the transmission time interval (TTI), including two time slots, each lasting 0.5 ms [DON 10].

The radio resources available for users are called resource blocks (RBs), which are defined in the frequency and time domains. In the frequency domain, one RB is a collection of 12 contiguous sub-carriers and each RB consists of 180 kHz bandwidth (12 sub-carriers; each subcarrier is 15 kHz), as shown in Figure 4.2, whereas in the time domain, each RB has 0.5 ms time slot, each of which carries seven OFDM symbols, as shown in Figure 4.3. Two consecutive time domain RBs make a TTI, which is equal to one sub-frame of 1 ms duration. Each UE reports its channel condition to its corresponding eNodeB on every TTI, which includes the received signal-to-noise ratio (SNR) of each sub-carrier at the user side. These feedback reports also consist of other radio parameter statuses perceived by the UE, such as CQI, MOS, Rank Indicator and user buffer status.

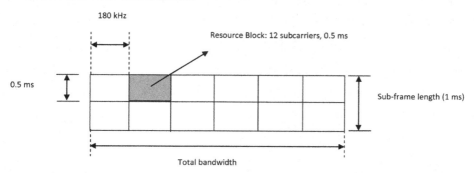

Figure 4.2. *LTE frame structure in frequency domain*

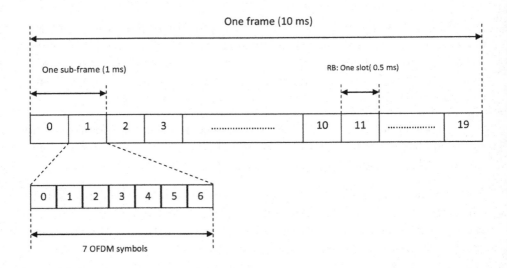

Figure 4.3. *LTE frame structure in time domain*

4.3. E-model

The E-model defined in the ITU-T Rec. G. 107 [INT 11] is an analytical model of voice quality which is used for network planning purposes. In the E-model, the main objective is to calculate the R-factor, which measures the voice quality ranging from 100 to 0, where 100 is the best quality and 0 is the worst quality. The R-factor value is used to determine the MOS value, which is the arithmetic average of user opinion. The MOS value is obtained from the R-factor using equation [4.1] [UEM 08]:

$$MOS = \begin{cases} 1 & R < 1 \\ 1 + 0.035R + R(R - 60)(100 - R)7.10^{-6} & 0 < R < 100 \\ 4.5 & R > 100 \end{cases} \quad [4.1]$$

The general correlation between the R-factor, MOS scores and the quality of user experience with VoIP service is shown in Table 4.1. A high value of the R-factor gives the highest MOS, and the user gets the best QoS with high satisfaction experiences.

R-Factor (lower limit)	MOS (lower limit)	User experience
90	4.34	Excellent
80	4.03	Good
70	3.60	Fair
60	3.10	Poor
50	2.58	Bad

Table 4.1. *Correlation between R-Factor, MOS and user experience*

The R-factor mainly depends on four parameters, as shown in equation [4.2]:

$$R = R_o - I_s - I_d - I_{ef} + A \qquad [4.2]$$

where R_o represents the basic signal-to-noise ratio, which includes noise sources such as circuit and room noise; I_s is a combination of all impairments with voice signal; I_d is the impairment's factor caused by delay; I_{ef} is an effective equipment impairment factor associated with the losses as it is defined in [INT 01b] and A is the advantage factor. In [INT 07b], ITU-T provides the common values of impairment factors. After selecting the default values, we can obtain the reduced expression for the R-factor in equation [4.3]:

$$R = 94.2 - I_d - I_{ef} \qquad [4.3]$$

Equation [4.3] clearly shows that the R-factor mainly depends on the end-to-end delay and total loss probability, which affect the VoIP call quality. The delay component (I_d) is provided in [INT 11], and its influence on voice quality depends on a critical time value of 177.3 ms, which is the total delay budget for VoIP streams. The impact of this delay is modeled in [COL 01] and given in equation [4.4]:

$$I_d = 0.024d + 0.11(d - 177.3)H(d - 177.3) \qquad [4.4]$$

where d is the one-way delay (in ms) and $H(x)$ is a step function as mentioned in equation [4.5]:

$$H(x) = \begin{cases} 0 & \text{if } x < 0 \\ 1 & \text{if } x \geq 0 \end{cases} \qquad [4.5]$$

The quality of a VoIP call also depends on loss impairment (I_{ef}), as is clearly shown in equation [4.3]. In order to find the expression for calculating the value of I_{ef}, we use the methods proposed in [COL 01, DIN 03, SEN 06] that calculate the overall packet loss rate as

$$I_{ef} = \gamma_1 + \gamma_2 ln(1 + \gamma_3 e) \qquad [4.6]$$

where e is the total loss probability (including network and buffer), which has a value between 0 and 1; γ_1 represents the voice quality impairment factor caused by the encoder and γ_2 and γ_3 represent the impact of loss in voice quality for a given codec. In the case of a G.729-A codec, $\gamma_1 = 11$, $\gamma_2 = 40$ and $\gamma_3 = 10$, whereas for a G.711 codec, $\gamma_1 = 0$, $\gamma_2 = 30$ and $\gamma_3 = 15$, as presented in [COL 01]. Using the G.729-A codec, the final expression of the R-factor is given in equation [4.7]:

$$R = 94.2 - 0.024d - 0.11(d - 177.3)H(d - 177.3) - 11 - 40ln(1 + 10e) [4.7]$$

4.4. DRX mechanism

The DRX mechanism has already been implemented on 2G (GSM) and 3G (UMTS) cellular networks. LTE specification has adopted DRX at the link level to save power and extend battery life of the UE. In LTE networks, the DRX mechanism can observe the Radio Resource Control (RRC) states between the UE and eNodeB [ETS 12]. The RRC has two different states where the DRX mechanism can be worked: RRC_Idle and $RRC\_Connected$.

In the RRC_Idle state, the UE is registered in the LTE network with a specific unique identifier, but it does not have an active session with the eNodeB. In this state, the eNodeB can page the UE at any time for different purposes (e.g. get location information), whereas the UE can request an uplink channel by establishing a $RRC\_Connected$ state, so that it can receive and transmit data. In the $RRC\_Connected$ state, the DRX mode can be enabled during idle periods between the packet arrivals. If there is no data packet, the UE can go into DRX mode.

In the LTE's DRX mechanism, the sleep/wakeup scheduling of each UE receiver could be described in terms of three periods (ON-Duration, Inactivity and Sleep Interval), as shown in Figure 4.4. The values of LTE's DRX parameter are defined in [ETS 12]. In this chapter, we consider the following parameters:

– DRX cycle: the time interval between the start of two consecutive ON-Duration periods, in which the UE remains active. One DRX cycle consists of an ON-Duration and a Sleep Interval.

– ON-Duration (t): the time when the UE is in the active state and listens to the physical downlink control channel (PDCCH). If any data packet is scheduled, the UE starts its Inactivity Timer (t_I), otherwise it continues its DRX Sleep cycle. In this chapter, we set the value of this timer to 1 ms.

– Inactivity Timer (t_I): during ON-Duration, if a data packet is found through PDCCH, the UE starts its t_I and receives data packets. During t_I, if another PDCCH packet arrives, then the Inactivity time restarts itself. When t_I expires, the DRX cycle starts with a Sleep Interval. The value of t_I is set to 5 ms.

– Sleep Interval: it is a time interval during which the UE is in either the DRX Light Sleep t_{DS} mode (consumes less power) or the DRX Deep Sleep t_{DL} mode (consumes no power). In the Deep Sleep mode, the duration of a Sleep Interval is longer than that in the Light Sleep mode. We consider the following values of Light Sleep duration: 2, 5, 10, 16 and 20 ms; and Deep Sleep duration: 10, 20, 42, 64 and 80 ms, according to [ETS 12].

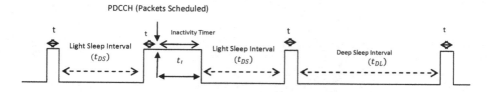

Figure 4.4. *LTE DRX mechanism at UE*

In [ETS 07], a semi-Markovian model is presented to determine the numerical values of power saved by the UE in the DRX mechanism, as shown in Figure 4.5, which is also used by [ZHO 08a, AHO 11, FOW 11]. This model shows that when the UE is in the active state and downloads data, it consumes 0.5 W/TTI. However, if the UE is in the Light Sleep mode, then it consumes 0.011 W/TTI, which means it saves 0.489 W/TTI, but in the case of the Deep Sleep mode, the UE does not utilize any power (i.e. 0 W/TTI), representing the full power-saving mode.

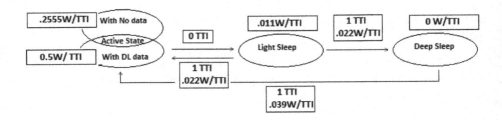

Figure 4.5. *Semi-Markovian model for power consumption*

The impact of the Light Sleep cycle and the Deep Sleep cycle on power saving can be observed in Figure 4.6. The power-saving behavior shown in Figure 4.6 is increasing for both the DRX Light Sleep cycle and Deep Sleep cycle, which is because the sleep cycles have longer duration and we have fixed the ON-Duration. The longer DRX cycles translate into more effective sleep time per cycle, resulting in better power saving.

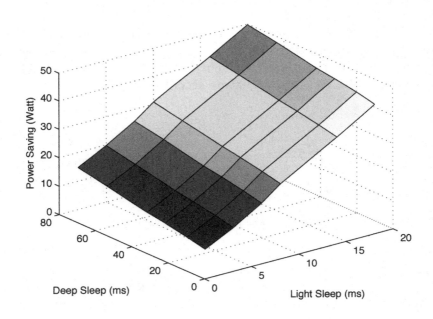

Figure 4.6. *Power saving during the Light and Deep Sleep cycles. For a color version of the figure, see www.iste.co.uk/mushtaq/systems.zip*

4.5. Methodology and implementation

Mostly, the algorithms and procedures specified for any wireless network are implemented and tested in the simulation environment, and their performances are evaluated at the link level and the system level. The link-level simulation environment considers only the link-related issues, such as MIMO gain, channel coding and decoding modeling and physical layer modeling required for system-level testing. However, the system-level simulation's environment examines system-level problems such as mobility handling, interference management and scheduling. The proposed work is implemented and tested in the LTE system-level simulator, which is developed in MATLAB® [IKU 10]. This simulator investigates the network performance by considering the physical layer results obtained from the link level. The simulator is implemented with object-oriented programming, which provides greater flexibility to modify, test and implement new functionalities in the current simulator.

The main advantage in separating the link-level and system-level simulators is the reduction of the complexity involved in each level. The link-level simulation is good in terms of developing receiver scenarios, feedback techniques, coding methods, etc. However, it is impractical for link-level simulations to consider the issues related to cell planning, scheduling and interference, which are part of system-level simulation. Similarly, it is impossible for system-level simulation to take care of the whole radio links between the UE and eNodeB, as it demands a large amount of computational power. The physical layer is implemented as a simple model in the system-level simulator, which acquires its significant properties with high accuracy but low complexity.

The LTE system-level simulator consists of two models: link measurement model and link performance model. The link measurement model measures the link quality information that is stored in trace files and later used for link adaptation and resource allocation. The signal-to-interference-and-noise ratio (SINR) is a key parameter of the wireless communication system to measure its link quality. However, the link performance model uses the link adaptation strategy to determine the block error ratio (BLER) with reduced complexity. The BLER is computed at the UE on the basis of resource allocation and the modulation and coding scheme (MCS). There are 15 different MCSs defined for LTE, which provide 15 Channel Quality Indicator (CQI) values, as presented in Table 4.2. These CQI values use different coding rates between 1/13 and 1 according to different modulation schemes. The link performance model outputs are stored in trace files, which contain throughput and error rates that are easily used to calculate their distributions.

CQI index	Modulation	Effective Coding rate= $\frac{c_r}{e_r}$ x 1024	Spectral Efficiency= $\frac{R_b}{B}$
0		out of range	
1	QPSK	78	0.1523
2	QPSK	120	0.2344
3	QPSK	193	0.3770
4	QPSK	308	0.6016
5	QPSK	449	0.8770
6	QPSK	602	1.1758
7	16QAM	378	1.4766
8	16QAM	490	1.9141
9	16QAM	616	2.4063
10	64QAM	466	2.7305
11	64QAM	567	3.3223
12	64QAM	666	3.9023
13	64QAM	772	4.5234
14	64QAM	873	5.1152
15	64QAM	948	5.5547

Table 4.2. *4-bit CQI index and MCS [ETS 10]*

4.5.1. *Traditional algorithms*

In general, the main goals of packet-scheduling algorithms in a wireless system are to maximize the throughput and fairness among the users. Two traditional methods can be used in the LTE network because they perform well in some QoS metrics according to the network conditions:

1) The Best CQI (BCQI) algorithm chooses the users which report the highest downlink SNR values to the corresponding eNodeB, thus utilizing the radio resources efficiently among the users with good channel conditions. On the contrary, users who experience bad channel conditions would never get resources. As a result, overall system throughput increases but it results in starvation of resources for some users, especially users far away from eNodeB. Thus, the BCQI algorithm performs well in terms of throughput but poor in terms of fairness among the users [RAM 09].

2) The Proportional Fair (PF) algorithm was proposed to achieve high throughput and fair resource distribution among the UE. It was originally developed to support non-real-time traffic in code division multiple access-high data rate (CDMA-HDR) systems. The scheduling strategies based on the PF algorithm focus on a trade-off between maximum average throughput and fairness.

4.5.2. Proposed QEPEM

The user's QoE is significantly influenced by the QoS parameters. However, there is always a trade-off between the QoS and power saving because the power-saving mechanism significantly affects the QoS such as delay. It is essential to have a method that considers the significant factors that influence the user's QoE for in-speech VoIP traffic. From this perspective, a new downlink-scheduling method is proposed that efficiently utilizes the power and keeps balance between QoS and power consumption, as well as considering their impact on the user's QoE. The proposed *QoE power efficient method (QEPEM)* uses an opportunistic scheduling approach that calculates the priorities of UEs and assigns resources to them. Some scheduling schemes achieve multi-user diversity by using an opportunistic approach for assigning the resources to UE by considering channel conditions. High system throughputs can be achieved by assigning resources only to UE that has a good channel condition; however, these techniques fail to fulfill fairness and the UE QoS requirements. To solve these problems, other parameters are required in order to balance between spectral efficiency and UE requirements. The QEPEM uses an opportunistic scheduling approach, which is based on the six important scheduling dependencies that have a greater impact on QoS and power-saving mechanism: MOS, channel condition (CQI), average throughput history, UE buffer status, GBR/non-GBR traffic and DRX status. The priority values for each resource block (RB) are estimated for every UE; the scheduler assigns an RB to a UE, the priority value of which is the highest among all other UE for that specific RB. A short description of each scheduling dependency is as follows:

1) UE MOS: each UE calculates its MOS based on the R-factor, which takes into account different factors like QoS parameters that include all kinds of delay (network, buffer, and codec), packet loss (network and UE's playout) and other UE impairment factors. The scheduler gives high priority to those

UEs for which QoE is decreasing due to a large delay (approaching a pre-defined threshold) of data residing in the eNodeB buffer; a longer waiting time in the buffer means a higher priority, which prevents packet loss and enhances QoE.

2) Channel condition: a scheduler estimates data rates and modulation schemes for each UE on every sub-band. Estimation is based on CQI reports sent by the UE in the uplink, which include information about downlink SINR.

3) Average throughput: the averaged data rate experienced by each UE for a time window. By keeping track of the UE throughput history, the scheduler will be able to give more resources to UE that was lacking in the past to fulfill their requirements and, as a result, fairness among the UE would also increase.

4) GBR/non-GBR: schedulers require treating RT and NRT services separately. GBR is an important parameter for RT-serviced UEs. If a UE experiences a data rate lower than that defined by the GBR, the scheduler must allocate more resources to that UE.

5) UE buffer status: every UE has a finite buffer length (equal to 100 packets) for storing the received packets. Packet losses can occur due to the insufficient space in a buffer. In the proposed algorithm, buffer length at the UE is assumed to be limited and the scheduler gives high priority to the UE that has more buffer space to avoid packet loss. Similarly, the UE that has fewer spare buffers would get low priority to minimize packet loss.

6) DRX status: DRX is an effective power-saving technique to prolong UE battery life. There is a trade-off between power conservation and QoS; more power saving results in higher transmission delays and packet losses. To address this issue, the proposed QEPEM algorithm considers DRX status to retain the delays within thresholds, according to QCI characteristics of LTE.

4.5.3. *Scheduler architecture*

The main entities involved in the downlink-scheduling algorithm are shown in Figure 4.7, in which eNodeB is shown on the left-hand side with Layer 1–Layer 3 and the UE is shown on the right-hand side. The information flows shown in Figure 4.7 with solid lines are used by both the traditional and proposed scheduling algorithms, whereas information flows shown by dashed lines are used only by the proposed QEPEM scheduling algorithm.

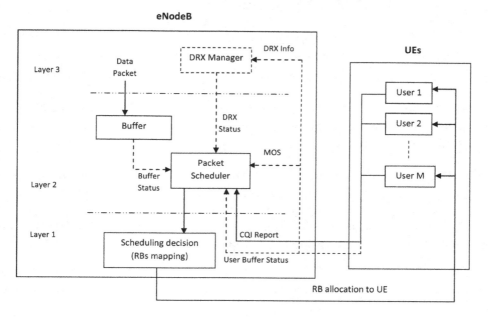

Figure 4.7. *Entities involved in the downlink packet scheduler*

The proposed scheduler at Layer 2 acquires CQI reports from the UE in order to estimate the channel conditions, while UE buffer statuses are also received to avoid packet loss because the receiver buffer at the UE is assumed to be limited. A set of buffers at the eNodeB stores the packets for each UE to be scheduled. The proposed scheduler attempts to minimize packet losses by prioritizing the UE that has the oldest packet in the eNodeB buffer. Each UE sends its MOS information to the packet scheduler, which represents the user-perceived quality, and DRX information to the DRX manager, which determines the remaining active and sleep mode time for each UE. The DRX manager sends the DRX status to the packet scheduler. By considering six scheduling dependencies, the QEPEM scheduler assigns resources to the UE through PDCCH. This allows the QEPEM scheduling algorithm to keep packets within delay bounds and effectively minimize packet delays and packet loss rate and maximize the user's QoE.

4.5.4. *Scheduling algorithm*

In this section, we describe our proposed QEPEM that selects and assigns available radio RBs to UE according to the priority matrix. The priority matrix is calculated by considering the six scheduling dependencies for each UE. The MOS is calculated from the R-factor, which considers all types of delay (network, buffer and codec) and packet loss (network and UE's playout) factors; as a result, the MOS represents the overall effect of delay and packet loss. The priority values for each RB are estimated for each UE; the scheduler assigns RB to a UE, the priority value of which is the highest among all other UE for that specific RB.

To calculate the priorities, the algorithm first estimates maximum achievable throughputs for every RB if assigned to UE according to channel conditions reported by UE. In order to balance between system throughput and fair resource distribution, the proposed scheduler (henceforth referred to as QEPEM) utilizes the property of Proportional Fair (PF), which is defined in [RAM 09]

$$fair\_factor_i = \frac{achievable\_throughput_{ij}}{average\_throughput_i} \qquad [4.8]$$

$$R_i(t) = \left(1 - \frac{1}{t_c}\right) * R_i(t-1) + \frac{1}{t_c} * r_i(t-1) \qquad [4.9]$$

In equation [4.8], $achievable\_throughput_{ij}$ represents a theoretically achievable throughput of RB_j if assigned to UE_i at every TTI. In equation [4.9], R_i represents the $average\_throughput_i$ of UE_i over a window t_c at every TTI and r_i is an achievable throughput of UE_i. The window size t_c is an important element, which is used to calculate the average data rate experienced by each UE.

The priority function P_{ij} calculates priorities of $Non-RealTime(NRT)$ and $RealTime(RT)$ services from Equations [4.10] and [4.11], respectively. In this study, RT VoIP is used to evaluate the proposed QEPEM; however, calculating the user perception (MOS) for different NRT

traffic can be considered in future work:

$$P_{ij} = MOS_i * \delta_i \left(fair\_factor_i \right), \quad i \text{ is } NRT \ UE \qquad [4.10]$$

$$P_{ij} = MOS_i * \delta_i \left(fair\_factor_i \left(\frac{GBR}{average\_throughput_i} \right)^{\varnothing} \right),$$

$$i \text{ is } RT\,UE \qquad [4.11]$$

where $\varnothing$ is a tunable exponential factor for GBR and δ is a DRX status indicator for each UE. P_{ij} is a priority matrix for each RB_j if assigned to UE_i while $fair\_factor_i$ is in accordance with equation [4.8]. GBR is the guaranteed bitrate requirement for GBR UE. The tunable exponential factor $\varnothing$ can be used to adjust the preferences of GBR UE; if a UE achieves a lower-than-average throughput required by GBR, the scheduler will increase the priority of that UE to fulfill the GBR requirement and vice versa. The MOS_i is a priority multiplier that increases the priority of UE facing the degradation of service due to delay and packet loss rate, as higher priority to prevent packet loss. The GBR is irrelevant to NRT traffic because NRT traffic is not delay-sensitive and it does not require minimum data rates to guarantee.

The QEPEM is designed in conjunction with the DRX mechanism to fully exploit the high bandwidth efficiency of LTE. The DRX manager at eNodeB shares DRX status with the UE. On each TTI, the scheduler must consider only the UE that is in an active mode of operation and then allocate resources for data transmission; this is achieved by including the DRX status in priority criteria. The DRX status δ defines the state of a UE, when it is in active mode $\delta = 1$. When a UE is in sleep mode, $\delta = 0$ takes that UE out of the scheduling competition. Thus, the scheduler helps reduce resource wastage by considering only the UE that is in active state.

4.6. Simulation setup

The simulation setup consists of an LTE network that is operating at 2 GHz operating frequency and 5 MHz system channel bandwidth. The eNodeB is considered to be static, which is serving 15 VoIP traffic UE that are uniformly distributed within the sector and allowed to move randomly. These UEs can be considered as pedestrians moving with a speed of 5 km/h. The VoIP traffic model is used to simulate the IP-based voice, according to [3GP 07]. The VoIP traffic model is considered due to the major usage on the UE. Additionally, fading models [CLA 05] and [INT 97] are used to simulate realistic channel conditions. DRX Light Sleep and Deep Sleep mechanisms are implemented on the UEs for saving power; on the contrary, each UE has a finite buffer length at eNodeB that buffered data when the UE is in sleeping mode.

A longer Deep Sleep duration can cause the buffer overflow of UE at the eNodeB because the number of packets being created would be much higher than those being scheduled. In this work, DRX ON-Duration and In-active parameters are set to 1 TTI and 5 TTIs, respectively, to avoid the UE buffer overflow at eNodeB. The power-saving effect on user's QoE is considered in terms of QoS parameters that will be presented and discussed, which are average system throughput, average throughput fairness index, packet loss rate (PLR) and average packet delay. The three performance evaluation parameters are well known; however, the Fairness Index can be defined in terms of system resource allocation or throughput. The Raj Jain equation is used to obtain a throughput fairness index. In [JAI 91], fairness index J for n UE is defined as

$$J(x_1, x_2, \ldots, x_n) = \frac{(\sum_{i=1}^{n} x_i)^2}{n \sum_{i=1}^{n} x_i^2} \qquad [4.12]$$

where x_i is the throughput for the ith UE. The best case can give a maximum value of 1, which means all UE achieved exactly the same throughput. When the difference between the UE throughput increases, the value of Jain's equation decreases. The important simulation parameters are listed in Table 4.3, and the durations of Light and Deep Sleep mode cycles are selected according to 3GPP TS 36.331 version 8.8.0 Release 8.

4.7. Performance analysis with a fixed Deep Sleep duration of 20 ms

The performance of the proposed QEPEM will be evaluated and compared with two traditional scheduling algorithms: Proportional Fair (PF) and Best CQI (BCQI) in power-saving mode. The evaluation and comparison are done in the same simulation environment and parameters.

The simulation setups are the same for all the schedulers as given in Table 4.3, and the performance is evaluated in the varying power-saving environment

DRX Light Sleep with fixed Deep Sleep mode of 20 TTIs (20ms). The DRX mechanism is applied to the UE together with the fixed DRX ON-Duration of 1 TTI, whereas the In-Active duration is set to 5 TTIs. The simulation executes for different Light Sleep parameters, and one result is given in Figure 4.8, while impacts of other parameters are summarized in Table 4.4.

Parameters	Values
eNodeB radius	250 m
Number of sectors per eNodeB	3
Target area	Single sector
Number of UEs	15
eNodeB total TX power	20 W
Number of antennas (SISO)	1 TX, 1 RX
Fading models	Fast fading
UE speed	5 km/h
Operating frequency band	2 GHz
System channel bandwidth	5 MHz
Number of RBs	25
$\varnothing$	2
GBR	25 kbps
CQI reporting	Every TTI
Traffic model	VoIP
VoIP packet generation interval	20 ms
VoIP delay threshold	100 ms
Power-saving mechanism	DRX Light and Deep Sleep
DRX on duration	1 TTI
DRX In-Active duration	5 TTIs
DRX Light Sleep duration	2, 5, 10, 16, 20 (ms)
DRX Deep Sleep duration	10, 20, 40, 64, 80 (ms)

Table 4.3. *Main simulation parameters*

Figure 4.8(a) shows average system throughput when the simulation runs for 5,000 TTIs, which is equal to 5 s. The results are obtained, when the duration of the DRX Light Sleep cycle is set to 20 ms (20 TTIs), with a fixed duration of the DRX Deep Sleep cycle, which is equal to 20 ms (20 TTIs). The result shows that the throughput of the proposed QEPEM is significantly higher than that of all the other schedulers. The QEPEM uses the DRX information of each UE; in other words, the QEPEM considers the ON-Duration and In-Active duration of all UEs during the scheduling decision. The traditional schedulers are designed to consider all the UE that is connected at the time scheduling is performed. PF holds second position in terms of throughput because it also tries to balance the throughput with the resource fairness. BCQI performed the worst in this regard because BCQI chooses only those UEs that have the best channel conditions in the uplink through the CQI feedbacks.

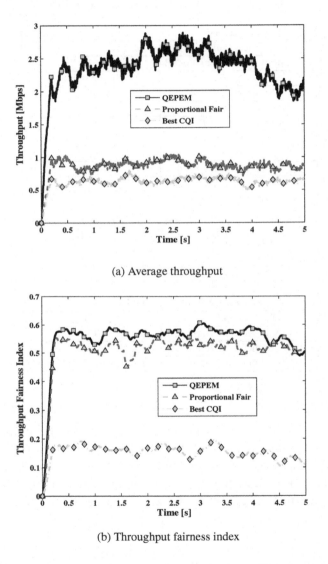

(a) Average throughput

(b) Throughput fairness index

Figure 4.8. *Light Sleep = 20 ms and fixed Deep Sleep = 20 ms*

Light	Scheduler	Throughput	F-Index	Delay	PLR	MOS
2	QEPEM	3.707	0.5894	9.8714	0	3.78
	PF	1.043	0.5350	17.6295	0.00059	3.86
	BCQI	1.566	0.1410	38.1408	0.4675	1.55
5	QEPEM	3.3865	0.6001	8.9632	0	3.66
	PF	1.0586	0.5362	17.3929	0.00043	3.87
	BCQI	1.3412	0.1470	33.8087	0.4494	1.55
10	QEPEM	2.6513	0.5393	10.5643	0.0024	3.75
	PF	1.0316	0.5385	17.8852	0	3.86
	BCQI	1.1071	0.1522	34.2655	0.4600	1.52
16	QEPEM	2.7837	0.5646	9.1295	0.0127	3.49
	PF	0.86255	0.4812	17.1979	0	3.87
	BCQI	0.7513	0.1523	36.6407	0.4634	1.53
20	QEPEM	2.3923	0.5617	10.7919	0.0013	3.87
	PF	0.8861	0.5191	19.4660	0	3.84
	BCQI	0.6382	0.1554	29.8075	0.4568	1.59

Table 4.4. *Evaluation of the schedulers at a fixed Deep Sleep cycle duration of 20 ms*

Figure 4.8(b) illustrates the Throughput Fairness Index according to Raj Jain's equation. The result clearly shows that the proposed QEPEM performed the best compared with all the other scheduling schemes. The QEPEM manages to achieve higher fairness because it considers the channel conditions and the UE's GBR requirements. It tries to allocate resources to UE in which packets are residing in the eNodeB buffer for a longer time to avoid packet losts and improve the user's QoE. Similarly if the UE is lacking in throughput according to the defined GBR requirement, then again more radio resources are allocated to that UE. PF does not consider the sleeping state of UE, but it tries to achieve fairness among them by considering the performance history of each set of UE. It follows the pattern of the QEPEM. The value of BCQI is close to the worst-case scenario, as it allocates the resources only to UE that reports good channel conditions.

Figure 4.9 illustrates the performance of three schedulers in terms of the user-perceived QoE, when DRX Light Sleep cycle has a duration of 20 ms together with fixed Deep Sleep duration of 20ms. Figure 4.9 shows that the QEPEM and PF have almost the same performance; however, BCQI shows the worst performance. Similarly, Figure 4.9 shows that the performance of PF is close to that of the proposed QEPEM, unless the Light Sleep duration is 16 ms. BCQI shows poor performance, as it deals only with the limited UE that reports the same channel quality.

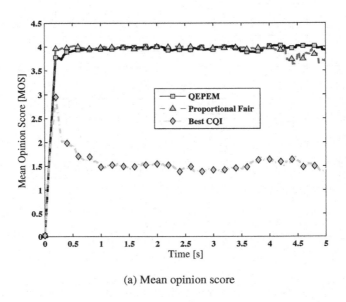

(a) Mean opinion score

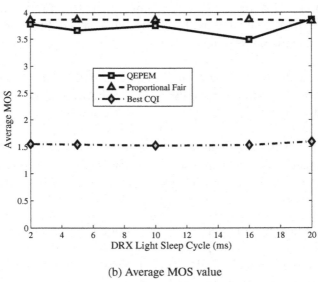

(b) Average MOS value

Figure 4.9. *Light Sleep = 20 ms and fixed Deep Sleep = 20 ms*

Table 4.4 summarizes the results of different Light Sleep cycles with a fixed Deep Sleep mode of 20 ms. The average values of distinctive performance parameters are given in terms of system throughput, throughput fairness index, packet delay, packet loss rate and user perception (MOS). The average value of packet delay shows that the QEPEM scheduler achieved the least delay followed by the PF scheduler, which outperformed the BCQI scheduler. When compared with the other methods, the proposed QEPEM performs best in terms of throughput, fairness index and delay. In terms of PLR and MOS, the QEPEM performs exceptionally better than BCQI, but sometimes its performance is close to that of PF. The BCQI scheduler shows the worst performance in all cases, as it assigns radio resources to limited UE.

Figure 4.10 shows the average throughput and fairness index for three scheduling methods: QEPEM, PF and BCQI. The results show the impact of DRX Light Sleep duration together with fixed Deep Sleep duration equal to 20 ms. Figure 4.10(a) shows that the QEPEM performs best because it is designed to provide best fairness among the UE by fulfilling the GBR UE requirements at the cost of lower system throughput. The results clearly represent that the QEPEM is least affected by the increase in sleep durations because it considers the DRX state of the UE and user perception in order to maximize the QoE. The performance of the BCQI and PF schedulers degrade significantly when the system works in power-saving mode. The figure shows that the QEPEM performance is superior to the other schemes when the duration of DRX sleep is increased. Figure 4.10(b) shows that the QEPEM outperforms the other methods, whereas the performance of PF is close to that of the proposed QEPEM. The BCQI performed the worst in this case due to its resource distribution policy.

Figure 4.11 illustrates the effect of power saving on packet delay, as shown in Figure 4.11(a), and packet loss rate, as shown in Figure 4.11(b), for the three scheduling methods. In the case of VoIP communication, it is required that when a packet is created, it must reach the UE within 100 ms, according to the QCI characteristic of LTE networks, otherwise the packet will be discarded. It is observed that when the duration of DRX Light Sleep increases, packets will encounter more delay because packet delay is directly proportional to the power being saved through the DRX sleep. Figure 4.11 shows that the QEPEM performs best followed by the PF method in terms of packet delay and packet loss rate. The results show that both schedulers follow a linear pattern. The QEPEM scheme is designed to reduce the packet delays and losses while achieving the high throughput and fairness to improve the user's QoE. BCQI performs worst in terms of packet delay and packet loss rate because it is designed to achieve maximum system throughput in normal operational mode without considering fairness and delay constraints.

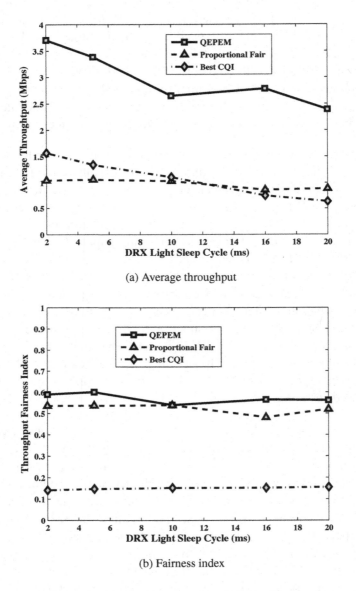

(a) Average throughput

(b) Fairness index

Figure 4.10. *Varied Light Sleep with fixed Deep Sleep = 20 ms*

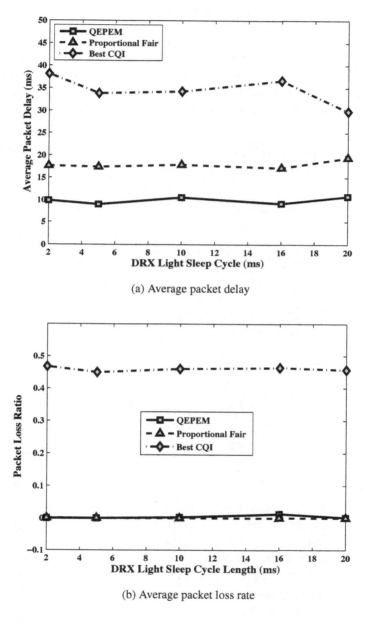

(a) Average packet delay

(b) Average packet loss rate

Figure 4.11. *Varied Light Sleep with fixed Deep Sleep = 20 ms*

4.8. Performance analysis with a fixed Light Sleep duration of 10 ms

The impact of a power-saving mechanism on user's QoE and QoS in LTE networks is evaluated by fixing the duration of the DRX Light Sleep cycle to 10 ms and observing the effect of different DRX Deep Sleep cycle durations. The impact of each Deep Sleep duration is evaluated and the results are summarized in Table 4.5.

Deep	Scheduler	Throughput	F-Index	Delay	PLR	MOS
10	QEPEM	3.5172	0.5838	5.7893	0	3.79
	PF	1.3473	0.5643	8.6391	0	3.78
	BCQI	1.2000	0.1549	32.2102	0.4103	1.55
20	QEPEM	2.6513	0.5393	10.5643	0.0024	3.75
	PF	1.0316	0.5385	17.8852	0	3.86
	BCQI	1.1071	0.1522	34.2655	0.4600	1.52
40	QEPEM	2.2174	0.5178	19.9674	0.0098	3.70
	PF	0.52386	0.4211	38.2932	0.0517	2.92
	BCQI	0.74179	0.1431	42.2722	0.5346	1.56
64	QEPEM	1.9751	0.4815	30.1797	0.0125	3.47
	PF	0.30250	0.2918	49.9616	0.3565	1.26
	BCQI	0.65989	0.1255	48.7677	0.6073	1.58
80	QEPEM	1.5037	0.4605	37.0972	0.0250	3.23
	PF	0.23113	0.2369	53.2352	0.4865	1.13
	BCQI	0.409880	0.1239	57.9616	0.6298	1.41

Table 4.5. *Evaluation of the schedulers at a fixed Light Sleep cycle duration of 10 ms*

Figure 4.12 shows average throughput and fairness index at a DRX Light Sleep cycle duration of 10 ms and a DRX Deep Sleep cycle duration of 80 ms. The QEPEM shows the best performance in terms of throughput and fairness compared with the other scheduling schemes due to its efficient scheduling decision-making, which is based on important parameters (e.g. DRX, MOS and GBR). In addition, PF outperforms the traditional BCQI scheme. By increasing the duration of the Deep Sleep cycle, the average throughput of all the scheduling schemes is reduced. Figure 4.12(a) shows that the QEPEM again achieves the highest throughput because it assigns the resources to UE that is in active mode, which results in high fairness index as shown in Figure 4.12(b).

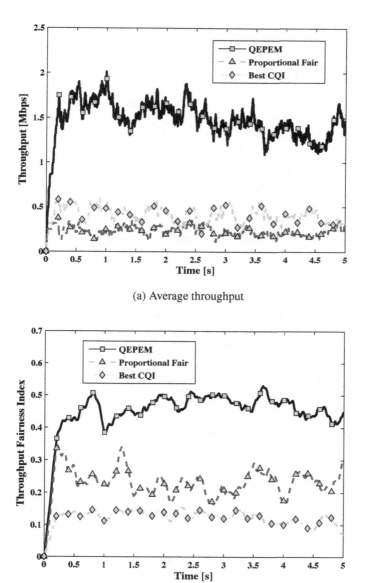

(a) Average throughput

(b) Throughput fairness index

Figure 4.12. *Deep Sleep = 80 ms and fixed Light Sleep = 10 ms*

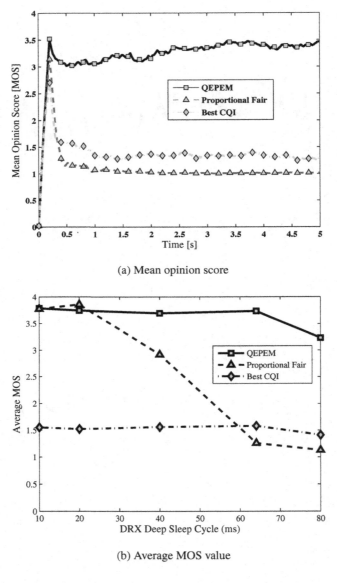

(a) Mean opinion score

(b) Average MOS value

Figure 4.13. *Deep Sleep = 80 ms and fixed Light Sleep = 10 ms*

Figure 4.13 shows the user-perceived QoE in the form of MOS values while using the three scheduling methods, when the DRX Deep Sleep cycle duration is 80 ms and the fixed DRX Light Sleep cycle duration is 10 ms. Figure 4.13(a) clearly shows that the QEPEM achieves a high user satisfaction together with a high power saving at the UE. This is because the QEPEM considers user perception and DRX status while making the scheduling decision. BCQI shows the second-best performance, while PF shows the worst performance in this case scenario. Figure 4.13(b) presents the performance of the three scheduling methods using the average MOS performance metric. It is observed that when the duration of the Deep Sleep cycle is increased, the average MOS of PF is significantly reduced. The QEPEM again achieves the highest user satisfaction. BCQI shows a nearly identical behavior, as it serves only the limited UE that faces almost the same network quality.

Table 4.5 summarizes the performance of three schedulers, QEPEM, PF and BCQI, in the forms of QoS parameters (throughput, fairness index, packet delay and packet loss rate) that have a significant influence on the user-perceived QoE. When the duration of Deep Sleep cycles increase, the performances of all schedulers is degraded. However, the QEPEM has successfully managed the situation by considering the DRX and user perception in its scheduling decision. The QEPEM has the highest system throughput and fairness index and the least packet delay in comparison to the other schedulers, while in terms of PLR and MOS, the QEPEM again outperforms PF, except when the duration of Deep Sleep is 20 ms, where the QEPEM's performance is very close to that of PF. BCQI shows the worst performance in all case scenarios because it allocates the resources to fewer sets of UE by considering the channel quality.

Figure 4.14 shows the performances of the QEPEM, PF and BCQI in terms of QoS parameters, which are average throughput and fairness index. The system throughput is averaged over 5,000 TTIs for each scheduler. The QEPEM performs better than the other traditional schemes (PF and BCQI) in terms of both performance parameters. In the power-saving mode, the performances of PF and BCQI degraded significantly in their respected order. The result clearly shows that the QEPEM still outperforms the other schemes when the duration of the DRX Deep Sleep is increased. When the DRX Deep Sleep duration is increased continuously, as shown in Figure 4.14, the QEPEM has the highest performance index, but the PF experienced a poor system throughput, as indicated by Figure 4.14(a). Similarly, the performance of PF significantly degrades when the Deep Sleep duration exceeds 20 ms, as shown in Figure 4.14(b).

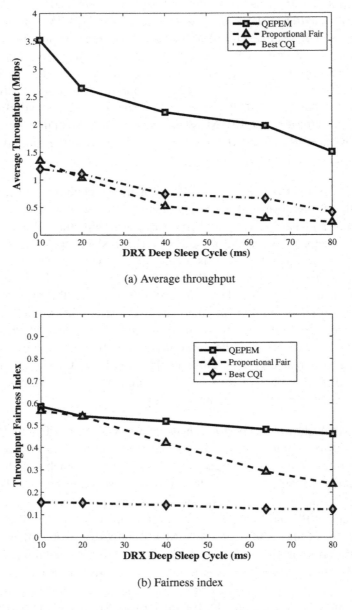

(a) Average throughput

(b) Fairness index

Figure 4.14. *Varied Deep Sleep with fixed Light Sleep = 10 ms*

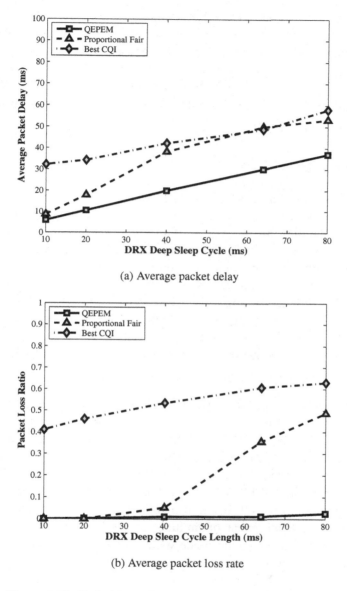

(a) Average packet delay

(b) Average packet loss rate

Figure 4.15. *Varied Deep Sleep with fixed Light Sleep = 10 ms*

Figure 4.15 shows the performance of the three schedulers in terms of packet delay and loss rate. When the Deep Sleep duration increases, result packets start to get delayed, as the packet delay is directly proportional to the power being saved through the DRX Deep and Light Sleep durations. The simulation results clearly show that the QEPEM performs best with less packet delay, as indicated in Figure 4.15(a), and with low packet loss rate, as shown in Figure 4.15(b). The performance of PF is significantly affected, as it has a high packet loss rate when the duration of Deep Sleep increases from more than 40 ms. The BCQI shows the worst performance in terms of both packet delay and packet loss rate due to its resource allocation policy.

4.9. Conclusion

In this chapter, we discussed the general aspects of LTE wireless networks. The main focus was to develop a downlink-scheduling algorithm that manages the RT multimedia VoIP traffic by considering distinct significant parameters. The resource allocation process mainly depends on different scheduling parameters that play an important role in scheduling decisions for achieving the desired QoS objective and high user satisfaction. In the proposed QEPEM algorithm, the main challenge was to acquire the user-perceived QoE for in-speech VoIP traffic, which is possible by using the E-model. The E-model is an analytical model of voice quality, which is used to determine the MOS value calculated as the arithmetic average of user opinion.

The proposed QEPEM for LTE downlink scheduling uses the opportunistic scheduling approach for delay-sensitive multimedia traffic (VoIP). It takes into account the six important scheduling dependencies that have a greater impact on QoS and QoE: user's MOS, channel condition (CQI), average throughput history, UE buffer status, GBR/non-GBR traffic and DRX status. The QEPEM opts to enhance the QoE and provides better QoS by decreasing packet losses, improving fairness between UE and meeting the QoS requirement of multimedia services. It has the ability to assure QoS in the power-saving mode with a high level of user satisfaction. The QEPEM maximizes the user's QoE using user perception in its scheduling decision. The performance of the QEPEM is compared with that of the traditional schemes based on different QoS attributes using simulations. The simulation results show that PLR has a higher influence on QoE compared with delay. The QEPEM was evaluated in the power-saving mode, and the impact of power saving on QoS and QoE was also examined. In the power-saving environment, the QEPEM performed remarkably better than the traditional schedulers with better user experience because it allocated resources efficiently and fairly between UE.

QoE and Power-saving Model for 5G Network

In Chapter 4, we focused on the 4G (LTE-A) network from the perspective of QoE-based power-efficient downlink-scheduling algorithm. The proposed scheduler allocates the resources to user equipment (UE) by considering the six important parameters, including user's QoE, and evaluates the impact of power saving on QoS and QoE using delay-sensitive VoIP traffic. This chapter focuses on two main aspects of 5G networks: (i) QoE using multimedia services (VoIP and video) and (ii) power-saving model for mobile device and virtual base station (VBS). First, we shall describe a method that minimizes the overall network delay for multimedia services: constant bitrate (VoIP) and variable bitrate (video) traffic model. In addition, we propose a method that measures the user's QoE for video streaming traffic using the network QoS parameters: delay and packet loss rate. The performance of the proposed QoE method is compared with that of the QoV method, and it is found that the proposed QoE method performed best by carefully handling the impact of QoS parameters, as it successfully reduces the overall network delays, which results in maximizing the user's QoE. Second, we discuss a method that calculates the power consumption of a 5G network by considering its main elements based on the current vision of 5G network infrastructure. The proposed model uses the component-based methodology that simplifies the process by taking into account various high-power consuming elements. The proposed method is evaluated by considering the three UE's DRX models and VBS with respect to different DRX timers in terms of power saving (PS) and delay as performance parameters.

5.1. Introduction

The 4G standard Long-Term Evolution-Advanced (LTE-A) has been deployed in many countries. Now, technology is evolving toward the 5G standard, which is expected to start its service in 2020. The 5G cellular network will mainly focus on cloud computing, and Quality of Service (QoS) parameters (e.g. delay, loss rate) will mainly influence the cloud network performance. The impact of user-perceived Quality of Experience (QoE) using multimedia services and applications significantly relies on the QoS parameters. The key challenge of 5G technology is to reduce the delay to less than 1 ms.

Multimedia traffic will be the main challenge for a wireless communication system. It becomes important for the next-generation wireless networks (5G) to provide these multimedia services in an efficient way to meet the end-user's quality expectation. Cloud computing will be the fundamental part of 5G architecture that provides a powerful computing platform to support ultra-high-definition video services (e.g. Live IPTV, 2D/3D video, Video on Demand "VoD", Interactive gaming) to fulfill the demand of end-users.

Cloud computing is a computing paradigm in which configurable shared resources are available to fulfill the demand (e.g. applications, services, storage). The main features of cloud computing are on-demand self-service, resource pooling, broadband network access, rapid elasticity and measured service [PAL 10]. It contains three main service models: Infrastructure as a Service (IaaS), Platform as a Service (PaaS) and Software as a Service (SaaS). With the enormous advance in wireless communication, smart devices (e.g. Tablet, iPhone, Android, Windows) provide more flexibility to users via a cloud computing system. This new paradigm of cloud computing in mobile environment introduces the mobile cloud computing (MCC).

Mobile devices are still not sufficiently powerful, because they have limited computing capacity, storage and energy resources. MCC can effectively fill the gap between demanding computing power and mobile device limitations. It facilitates the mobile devices to offload the computing power and data storage demand into the powerful computing infrastructure of the cloud [CAI 14]. The future wireless 5G standards are still not completely finalized, but there are some key visionary elements that will evolve the technologies. The cloud-based radio access network (C-RAN) infrastructure is a novel cellular network architecture for 5G mobile networks that will provide shared on-demand computation, storage and network capacity wherever needed. In this chapter, terms like mobile device, user equipment and user are interchangeably used to mean the same context.

Conventionally, radio equipment such as remote radio unit (RRU) and baseband processing unit (BBU) is located within the cellular base station (BS). To improve the conventional method, the C-RAN has been introduced to manage hundreds to thousands of remotely distributed RRU that are connected to the centralized pool of BBUs. There are some significant advantages to changing from distributed to centralized baseband processing. Consolidation, pooling and virtualization of BBU resources lead to lower deployment cost by avoiding the redundant capabilities and over-commissioning. It also enables better load sharing, improved network performance via advanced processing techniques, equipment cost saving and, last but not the least, reduced power consumption.

In general, the performance of networks mainly depends on the network QoS parameters that play an important role in selecting the suitable server to improve user satisfaction. This chapter describes the C-RAN that provides multimedia video streaming and VoIP services to end-users. Network QoS parameters, such as delay and packet loss rate, are considered as the influencing factors of the user-perceived QoE. An analytical method is described that decreases the overall network delay. The proposed QoE method measures the user's QoE using the delay and packet loss rate for a video streaming service that considers the future needs of 5G. Among the different factors, the network QoS parameters directly influence the user-perceived QoE. The main objective is to satisfy the user's QoE by reducing the traffic delay that can cause dropping of video packets in a cloud network.

In this chapter, we also discuss the power-saving model for mobile devices and VBS in the 5G era. The power optimization of UE is a key challenge for any wireless communication system. Discontinuous reception (DRX) is an important mechanism to optimize the UE's power utilization in cellular networks, as it is already implemented in digital cellular networks (2G, 3G and 4G) with different DRX mechanisms. The objective of the DRX method is to sustain the UE battery life by monitoring the user's activities. The DRX power-saving method follows a simple process: it saves power by switching off (sleeping state) the UE transceiver when there are no transmitted data. However, the DRX sleep state considerably increases the packet delay.

The DRX method is expected to again play a key role in 5G networks in order to optimize the UE's power consumption. The UE power-saving mechanism in the 5G standard is not finalized, and from this perspective, we use the extended version of three-state DRX model of LTE-A to four-state DRX and five-state DRX models to evaluate its performance under different scenarios of the DRX mechanism together with VBS.

The VBS will be a key element in 5G network architecture, as it will significantly improve the network efficiency using the cloud-based infrastructure, which will consist of a large pool of computational resources (i.e. BBU) and allocate sufficient resources based on the demand. Therefore, each VBS will require different computational resources based on processing power demanded by the UEs. In this context, the power consumption of each VBS will fluctuate because the C-RAN dynamically allocates base-band computational resources.

In the second part of this chapter, we describe how the LTE-A three-state DRX model will be extended to four-state DRX and five-state DRX models. The performances of these DRX models are evaluated for 5G networks using the VBS. The impacts of extended DRX models are evaluated against the three-state DRX model with respect to PS factor and delay. In addition, the influences of the three DRX state models (three-state, four-state and five-state DRX models) are evaluated in terms of power consumed by the UE and VBS by considering the different parameters of DRX mechanism. To the best of our knowledge, this is the first study to consider the power consumption of the UE along with the VBS, as opposed to other studies that have generally focused on either the UE or the VBS.

5.2. QoE and 5G network

User satisfaction is one of the key elements that provide the network operators with the ability to sense the contribution of the network's performance to the overall customer satisfaction in terms of reliability, availability, scalability, speed, accuracy and efficiency. QoE based on QoS plays a vital role in achieving the business goals for both content service provider (CSP) and network service provider (NSP). The understanding of

QoE is important for business offerings (called Q-Biz), as it drives the business and satisfies the user's expectation by offering the required resources, which decreases churn. However, 5G network will be autonomous and self-optimizing in that it will sense (local QoE awareness), think (data analysis and machine learning) and react (routing) based on the network characteristics.

5.2.1. *Cloud-based future cellular network*

The details of technical approaches in the future 5G networks are still not clear, because 5G standards have not been fixed; however, many aspects are cleared, e.g. supporting a 1000-fold gain in capacity, connecting at least 100 billion devices and achieving 10 Gbps connection to an individual user [HUA 14a]. The core network will be based on cloud for both control purpose and data. Figure 5.1 illustrates the envisioned architecture of future cellular networks (5G) together with cloud computing infrastructure. In general, the traditional BS contains two fundamental radio equipment: RRU and BBU located on the tower. The RRU handles the air interface, and BBU deals with the data modulation and code processing by controlling the connection between UE and cell. The future 5G cellular network introduces the C-RAN infrastructure that shifts the distributed processing units (i.e. BBU) to centralized units. The BSs in C-RAN simplify the network architecture, because all signal-processing and decision-making are made by the *wireless cloud network*. The IP traffic splitter proxy is like a *system architecture evolution gateway (SAE-GW)* in the Long-Term Evolution (LTE) architecture, where the user's data packets are passed to the SAE-GW before sending to the Internet [FAR 12].

5.2.2. *Traffic model*

The network can be modeled as a graph $G(V, A)$, where V is the set of all vertices (e.g. in our case, UEs and eNodeBs), and A is the set of arcs (represents the possible wireless transmission between the vertices) in the network. Each vertex $v \in V$ and each $arc \in A$. An arc in A can be characterized as arc (i,j) with two parameters: (i) link service capacity and (ii) user's QoE, which can be modeled as a general queuing system. The model considers the link as an average data rate (λ_{ij}) and service capacity (μ_{ij}). The average link delay depends only on the traffic. We can categorize the traffic based on their characteristics as a short-range dependent (SRD) and long-range dependent (LRD). Examples of SRD traffics are VoIP traffic and constant bitrate (CBR) type. When the link traffic shows the behavior of SRD characteristics, we can model the link queuing delay as an exponential distribution together with parameter $\mu_{ij} - \lambda_{ij}$. The average network average delay T_1 can be calculated by using Little's formula [KLE 75]:

$$T_1 \cong \frac{1}{\lambda} \sum_{(i,j) \in A} \left[\frac{\lambda_{ij}}{\mu_{ij} - \lambda_{ij}} \right] \qquad [5.1]$$

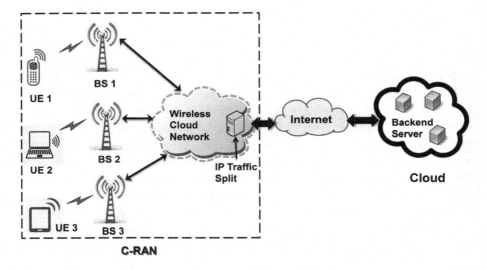

Figure 5.1. *Envisioned future cellular network architecture*

On the contrary, examples of LRD traffics include data traffic and variable bitrate (VBR). The behavior of link traffic in terms of LRD can be modeled using the fractional Brownian motion (fBm) queuing system. This queuing system has a heavy-tailed Weibull distribution [NOR 95]:

$$P_r (Q_{ij} > q) \approx exp \left(-\frac{(\mu_{ij} - \lambda_{ij})^{2H}}{2\kappa^2 (H) a\lambda_{ij}} q^{2-2H} \right) \qquad [5.2]$$

where $\kappa(H) = H^H(1-H)^{1-H}$, $H \in [0.5, 1)$ is the Hurst parameter and a is the index of dispersion. The network average delay (T_2) in the case of LRD traffic can be calculated by applying Little's formula:

$$T_2 \cong \tau \cdot \sum_{(i,j) \in A} \left[\frac{\lambda_{ij}}{(\mu_{ij} - \lambda_{ij})^{2H}} \right]^{\frac{1}{2-2H}} \qquad [5.3]$$

where $\tau = \Gamma(1 + \frac{1}{2-2H})[2\kappa^2(H)a]^{\frac{1}{2-2H}}$.

5.2.3. QoE modeling and measurement

Quality of Experience is subjective by nature, because of its relationship with user's viewpoint and its own concept of a "good quality". The ability to measure QoE would provide network operators with some sense of the contribution of the network's performance to the overall customer satisfaction, in terms of reliability, availability, scalability, speed, accuracy and efficiency. Many network researchers are now working on this concept and trying to integrate it in network decisions to ensure a high customer satisfaction with minimum network resources [MUS 14b]. The mean opinion score (MOS) is an example of a subjective measurement method in which users rate the service quality by giving five different point scores, from 5 to 1, where 5 is the best quality and 1 is the worst quality. MOS denotes discrete values, but the authors in [SHA 10] extended the discrete values and proposed the opinion score (OS) as a new QoE measurement scale that introduces a new value 0. According to the OS scale, quality can be classified as bad $\lfloor 0 - 1 \rfloor$, poor $\lfloor 1 - 2 \rfloor$, fair $\lfloor 2 - 3 \rfloor$, good $\lfloor 3 - 4 \rfloor$ and excellent $\lfloor 4 - 5 \rfloor$. First, it becomes necessary to identify precisely the factors that affect QoE.

The QoS mainly influences the UE's QoE, as many QoS parameters directly/indirectly contributed their impact on the user-perceived QoS. The main QoS parameters that affect the multimedia services are bandwidth, jitter, delay and packet loss rate. In the case of multimedia video streaming service, the bandwidth can be managed by selecting the suitable video codec, while jitter can be handled by configuring the buffer management of the UE's decoder. However, the delay and packet loss rate are two main QoS parameters that required to be handled in an efficient way in order to improve the user-perceived QoE. Delay is an essential parameter that can be caused by dropping of video packet. In general, when a packet arrives after the end of the threshold timer, it cannot be considered in real-time applications (e.g. video streaming) and is believed to be lost. We use the delay and packet loss rate as the key QoS parameters to compute the user's QoE.

Each link between eNodeB and UE has QoE parameters for each UE, which is computed based on QoS parameters (delay and packet loss rate). We model each link $(i,j) \in A$ as an arc of the graph that represents the UE's QoE based on QoS offered by different eNodeB serving in the region of interest. The quality of video streaming service, and QoS parameters (delay and packet loss) are correlated via exponential hypothesis. We proposed the QoE model that is based on the exponential hypothesis presented in [ARO 12] and [FIE 10], to calculate the user's QoE for video services given in equation [5.4]:

$$QoE_{(i,j)} = exp^{1.576 - (4.188 \times 10^{-4}) \times D - (5.766 \times 10^{-2}) \times PLR} \qquad [5.4]$$

where $QoE_{(i,j)}$ represents the user perception UE_i from the $eNodeB_j$, D represents the delay and PLR is the packet loss rate on that link. We randomly select some values of delay and packet loss rate and evaluate their impact on user's QoE using the proposed method, as illustrated in Figure 5.2.

5.3. Optimization models

An optimization model is described as the one that minimizes the overall network delay and maximizes the user's QoE.

5.3.1. *Network design*

We consider a network where each arc $(i,j) \in A(i,j)$ belonging to A has the packet sending cost and each vertex i in V has a value denoted as b_i, which depicts the demand or supply of that vertex. The network has a set of demands, which is shown by symbol S. Each demand $s \in S$ originates from one source node $o_s \in V$, and terminates at another node $t_s \in V$, and there is an amount of traffic associated with this link, denoted as b_s. It assumes that each arc $(i,j) \in A$ has capacity $\mu(i,j)$, which represents the maximum traffic flow on the arc; however, a lower bound $l(i,j)$ denotes the minimum amount of traffic flow that must flow on the arc. Each node or vertex $i \in V$ has some supply/demand that is denoted as an integer $b(i)$. If $b(i) > 0$, then node i is considered as a supply node; if $b(i) < 0$, the node is a demand node with a demand of $-b(i)$ and if $b(i) = 0$, the node will be a transshipment node. In our problem, the objective is to minimize the delay of traffic flow that can cause the packet to be lost and that tends to minimize the user's QoE.

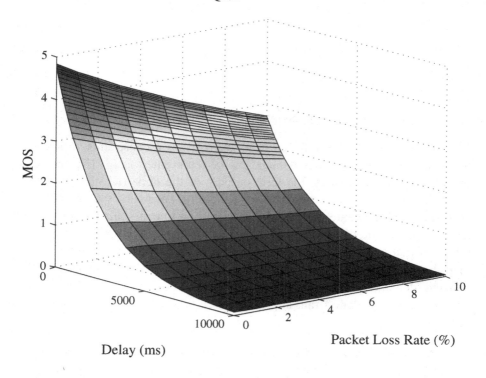

Figure 5.2. *Impact of delay and PLR on QoE. For a color version of the figure, see www.iste.co.uk/mushtaq/systems.zip*

Let us consider a network where a total of N links can be established. The problem can be formulated as follows:

$$min\ T1/T2 \tag{5.5}$$

subject to

$$\sum_{j:(i,j)\in A} f_{ij}^s - \sum_{j:(j,i)\in A} f_{ji}^s == \begin{cases} b_s, & i=o_s \\ -b_s, & i=t_s, s \in S \\ 0, & \text{otherwise} \end{cases} \quad [5.6]$$

$$l_{ij} \leq f_{ij}^s \leq \mu_{ij}, (i,j) \in A \quad [5.7]$$

$$0 \leq f_{ij}^s \leq y_{ij} * b_s, \ s \in S, (i,j) \in A \quad [5.8]$$

The above constraints can be interpreted as follows.

Constraint 5.6 can be referred to as mass balance constraints, where the link's flow in terms of supply/demand can be represented as f_i^s. The first term in the constraint represents the total outflow of the node (i.e. the total flow emitting from the node), whereas the second term shows the total inflow of a node (i.e. total flow entering the node). According to mass balance constraint, the supply/demand of the node must be equal to the total outflow minus total inflow of that node. If a node is the origination of the demand (supply node), then its outflow exceeds its inflow (b_s); if a node is the termination of the demand (demand node), then its inflow exceeds its outflow (i.e. $-b_s$) and if the node is an intermediate (transshipment node), then its outflow is equal to its inflow (i.e. 0).

Constraint 5.7 is referred to as flow bound constraints, where the flow $f_{i,j}^s$ must fulfill the link lower bound and capacity constraints. It allows the traffic flow within a certain range. In general, the lower bounds on arc flows have zero value.

Constraint 5.8 shows that if there is flow passing on $arc(i,j)$, then that $arc(i,j)$ should be selected. The variable y_{ij} represents the link (i,j) and is either established or not. When the link (i,j) is established then y_{ij} will be 1, otherwise it will be 0.

5.3.2. QoE

In cloud computing network, the UE's QoE mainly represents the quality provided by the server among different cloud servers. The UE's QoE can be calculated based on the QoS parameters (e.g. delay, packet loss rate) of the traffic flow (e.g. video), which represents the user satisfaction level. We consider a cellular network where the region of interest contains eNodeBs and serves the available UEs within its area. In future 5G cellular networks, the C-RAN will dynamically allocate the radio resource to serve the UE. In this context, UE satisfaction is very important, because the network QoS provided by the server can significantly influence the UE's QoE. User satisfaction will be a key factor in 5G networks, and giving power to a user for selecting the appropriate server in the C-RAN based on user's QoE will achieve this goal.

Let that the network coverage has UE_i users at location i, and it is considered that location must be finite. It is necessary for location i to have some QoE value in order to assign to the established connection eNodeB j. Based on the current QoS parameters, we consider that QoE is computed before assigning the UE to other eNodeB. The eNodeB ($s'j$) can serve u_j UE. The goal is to assign UE to eNodeB based on the QoE and minimize the cost associated with the link (i, j). Instead of describing the general model formally, we consider a simple model ingredient based on Figure 5.3.

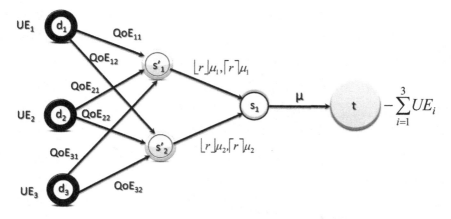

Figure 5.3. *Network diagram*

Each location i has the node as d_i and each cell j represents as a node s'_j. The decision variable is the QoE value at location i that is computed from serving QoS parameters from cell j, and it is represented by an $arc(i, j)$, e.g. from node d_i to node s'_j. We connect each s'_j node to s_j node, while flow through the arc must satisfy the lower and upper bounds of limit of the $arc(s'_j, s_j)$ that is equal to $(\lfloor r \rfloor \mu_j, \lceil r \rceil \mu_j)$, where $\lfloor r \rfloor$ represents a lower bound and $\lceil r \rceil$ represents the upper bound. Finally, it is necessary to consider the constraint that node j has service capacity μ_j.

5.4. Results

The performance of the proposed QoE method is compared with that of the QoV method [ARO 12] to calculate the user's QoE for video streaming together with the described analytical methods for the delay. The network delay is calculated for both SRD (CBR) and LRD (VBR) traffic models. In the case of SRD, we consider the VoIP traffic, while video streaming traffic is used for LRD by selecting the a half of link capacity $(a = \mu/2)$ with $H = 0.7$, and $\lambda = 693$. The link serving capacity is $\mu = 50$ Mbps for both the traffic models.

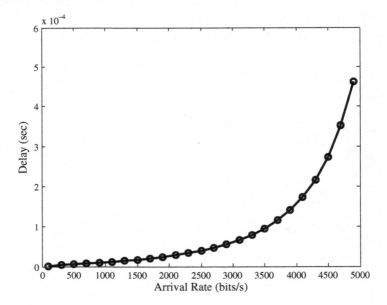

Figure 5.4. *Video delay*

Figure 5.4 shows the influence of different packet arrival rates on the overall network delay using video streaming traffic. It can be observed that when the packet arrival rates increase, the delay also increases, but the delay value is still very low (less than 1 ms) and does not degrade the network performance to a great extent. One of the key challenges of 5G network is to keep the network delay less than 1 ms in order to support real-time mobile control and vehicle-to-vehicle application and communication. The user's QoE is calculated using the proposed method (see equation [5.4]) based on these delay values. It should be noted that the overall QoE is always rated in the excellent scale (MOS > 4).

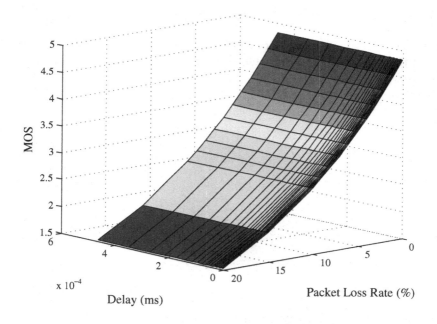

Figure 5.5. *Proposed QoE method: impact of delay and PLR on QoE. For a color version of the figure, see www.iste.co.uk/mushtaq/systems.zip*

The proposed QoE method is also evaluated by considering the QoS parameters in terms of delay and packet loss rate (PLR). Figure 5.5 illustrates the impact of delay and PLR on users' QoE using the video streaming traffic. Based on delay values as shown in Figure 5.4, the users' QoE is always high, and it is approximately MOS = 4.8 when there is not any PLR. Let us consider that some packets are dropped due to limitation of the user device. The possible causes can be buffer (*overflow/underflow*), insufficient memory, lack of system resources to process the packets, etc. Under these circumstances, the impact of delay and different values of PLR on the user-perceived quality experience is measured and presented in Figure 5.5. The increase in PLR also decreases the user's QoE, and when PLR = 20%, the user's QoE in terms of MOS is 1.5.

Figure 5.6 illustrates the impact of delay and packet loss rate on the QoV method using the video streaming traffic. The result clearly shows that QoV method does not properly tackle the packet loss rate, because our analytical method reduces the overall network delay, as shown in Figure 5.4. The maximum user's QoE in terms of MOS is 2.8 when the network delay is zero and PLR is also 0%. However, when PLR increases, it starts reducing the user satisfaction, and when $PLR = 20\%$, the user's QoE value is MOS = 1.

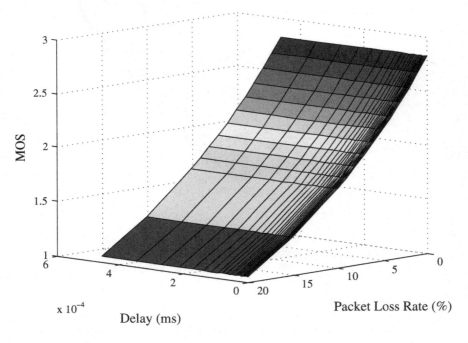

Figure 5.6. QoV method: impact of delay and PLR on QoE. For a color version of the figure, see www.iste.co.uk/mushtaq/systems.zip

Figure 5.7 depicts an impact of PLR on the proposed QoE method and the QoV method, when delay is zero. The result clearly shows that the proposed QoE method performs better than the QoV method. The proposed QoE method has MOS = 4.8, while QoV has MOS = 2.8 when PLR = 0%. However, QoV has MOS = 1 when PLR = 20%, but the proposed method has MOS = 1.5, because high PLR badly affects the user satisfaction [MUS 14a].

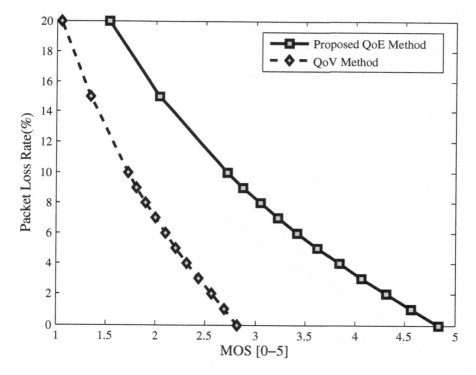

Figure 5.7. *Proposed QoE method versus QoV method*

Figure 5.8 shows how the different packet arrival rates affect the overall network delays using the VoIP traffic. The result clearly depicts that increase in packet arrival rate also increases the delay, but still all the delay values are very low and do not significantly decrease the network performance. When the network delay is very low, as in our case, the user's QoE will be at a maximum level for VoIP traffic, because it is a delay-sensitive traffic. In LTE-A, the network delay budget for VoIP is 100 ms [MUS 15]. In general, the VoIP traffic model generated the voice packet after each 20 ms [3GP 07]. To the best of our knowledge, we did not find an appropriate method in the literature to analyze the impact of PLR on user's QoE. The E-model method proposed by ITU-T Rec. G.107 [INT 11] is used to calculate the transmission rating factor (R-factor) for evaluating the voice quality. Based on the E-model, the methods proposed in [MUS 14b, UEM 08] and [DIN 03] are not valid for a very low delay.

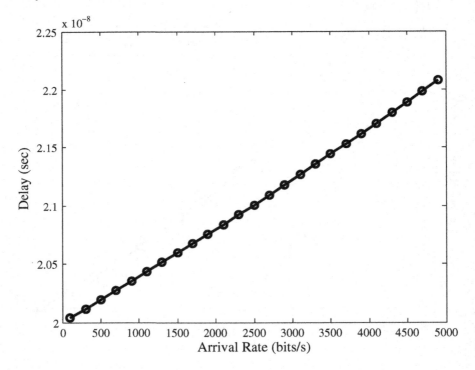

Figure 5.8. *VoIP delay*

5.5. Power-saving mechanism for UE and VBS

5.5.1. *User equipment (UE)*

Researchers have used different methodologies to measure the overall power consumption of UE and BS. In the case of UE, one way is to consider the different factors of hardware components (e.g. CPU, screen, SD card), wireless networks (e.g. WiFi, Bluetooth, ZigBee, 2G, 3G) and applications (e.g. video, voice) of the UE in order to measure an overall energy consumption. Most of these approaches were used to develop the power consumption model in order to estimate the power used by different components, as demonstrated in [CAR 10, PER 09, BAL 09, XIA 10, ZHA 10, SHY 09, ANA 09, ZHO 10].

Some methods use the various states of UE (idle, connected and power saving) in order to develop the power consumption model [LAU 14]. In [LAU 13], the authors developed a power model for smartphone. It considered the DRX operation together with cell bandwidth, screen and CPU power consumption of UE using the simulator, but focused only on UE. The DRX method uses two cycles in the UMTS [YAN 05]: DRX cycle for UE sleep (OFF) and inactivity cycle (ON) for wake-up. The LTE-A system enhanced the DRX method compared with the early DRX method, by allowing the UE to move into a sleep state even if the traffic buffer is not empty [FOW 12]. The DRX power-saving method in LTE-A depends on the scheduling, as it extends the UE's active time by re-initializing the DRX inactive timer [MUS 16]. The main purpose of DRX is to prolong the UE battery life in order to avoid the quick draining of UE power. In the next-generation wireless communication system (i.e. 5G), the DRX power-saving mechanism will be an important technique to optimize the UE battery life.

In Chapter 4, we discussed the scheduling method, *QoE power efficient method (QEPEM)*, for LTE-A. It optimized the UE power using the DRX Light and Deep Sleep cycle for maximizing the user-perceived service quality. In addition, we investigated the impact of different durations of DRX Light and Deep Sleep cycles on QoS of VoIP and their influence on end-users as well. In this chapter, the DRX mechanism of LTE-A is divided into three states of the DRX model using the semi-Markov process, as done in [MIH 10, ZHO 08a] and illustrated in Figure 5.9. Based on the Markov chain process, the state transition probability p_{ij} is obtained, where $i, j \in \{1, 2, 3\}$. Figure 5.9 implies the three DRX states: active state, light-sleep state and deep-sleep state, which are represented by state 1 (S_1), state 2 (S_2) and state 3 (S_3), respectively. Here, we extend the three-state DRX model to four-state and five-state models by adding the additional active states to light-sleep and deep-sleep states for optimizing the power usage at the UE. These additional active states have short ON periods (listening period) during which UE listens to the physical downlink control channel (PDCCH) and if the packets are scheduled, then UE downloads it and later moves to sleep state (OFF period). In our proposed method, the UE's power consumption is based on different states of the DRX mechanism and is calculated using Figure 5.10.

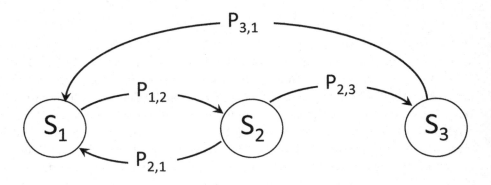

Figure 5.9. *DRX model with three states*

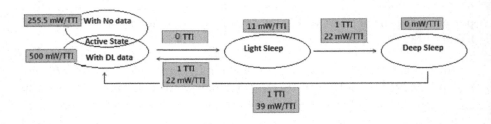

Figure 5.10. *Semi-Markov reference model for power consumption*

5.5.2. *Base station*

Most works in the literature focus on either the UE or BS. In [ARA 14], the authors proposed a method to minimize the power consumption of UE with guaranteed required throughput in the heterogeneous network. The proposed method considered both the BS and UE, but it is based on assigning the UEs to different BSs in order to reduce the total power consumption of

UE. In [ZHA 14], the authors proposed a computational-resource-aware energy consumption model for the VBS, but the model did not consider the power consumption at the UE. It used the component based on the EARTH model [AUE 11] in order to propose the power consumption model of the VBS. In [AUE 11], the authors proposed the EARTH model to compare the energy efficiency of different design approaches for wireless communication networks. It mainly focused on the energy efficiency of various BSs (e.g. femto, pico, macro) and did not consider the UE. It used the elementary approaches to calculate the total power consumption of BS by considering the different components. We proposed the power consumption method for the VBS that uses the component-based approach of [AUE 11] in order to calculate the power consumed by distinct elements of the VBS.

5.6. Energy consumption model

Researchers have proposed different methods to enhance the energy efficiency by considering the various elements of wireless networks. In general, wireless cellular networks consist of three main elements: BS, user mobile device and the core network. BS sites are primary elements in cellular communication networks, which consume 80% of energy required for any operational mobile cellular network [FEH 11]. This chapter considers the critical factors of BS and user mobile device that cause energy consumption from the perspective of 5G cellular networks.

5.6.1. *Virtual base station*

The energy efficiency of mobile cellular systems is highly based on BSs, as they consume a lot of energy to carry out the required computation. The EARTH model [AUE 11] is widely used in the literature, as it provides the energy consumption modeling for conventional BS [JIA 12, WU 13]. The general expression of the EARTH model is defined in equation [5.9]:

$$P_{in} = \begin{cases} N_{TRX}\left(P_0 + \Delta_p\,P_{out}\right), & 0 < P_{out} \leq P_{max} \\ N_{TRX}\,P_{sleep}, & P_{out} = 0 \end{cases} \qquad [5.9]$$

where P_{in} is the total power consumption of the BS, P_{out} represents the output power of each RF antenna which is measured at the input of RF antenna, P_0 is the minimum possible power consumption during non-zero load, N_{TRX} denotes the number of antennas at BS, Δ_p is the slope of power consumption that relies on load and P_{sleep} represents the power consumption during sleeping mode. When there is no transmission data scheduled, turning off various components of the BS will significantly save energy [MUS 16], especially during low-load periods (e.g. at night-time).

Future 5G mobile cellular network architecture will be based on the VBS, as it significantly reduces the communication cost and improves the network efficiency via a remote radio-based cloud infrastructure. Traditionally, the main parts of radio equipment, such as RRU and BBU, reside within the cellular BS. However, the future 5G mobile networks will be based on the C-RAN infrastructure, where the C-RAN will manage the remotely distributed RRUs, which will be connected with a centralized pool of BBUs. A BBU can communicate with other BBUs within the pool of BBUs, and energy consumption of BBUs for each BS will fluctuate, as the required base-band computational resources are dynamically allocated by the C-RAN. The EARTH model cannot be directly used to compute the energy efficiency of the VBS, as the number of dynamically allocated BBUs will reside on the C-RAN. The cloud-based cellular infrastructure requires a new energy consumption model for the VBS, as the widely used EARTH model was designed for conventional BS, which did not consider the variation of required base-band computational resources.

The EARTH model uses the component-based methodology to calculate the energy consumption of a BS. Taking advantage of the component-based strategy of the EARTH model, we calculate the power consumption of the VBS by calculating the power consumptions of the BBU and RRU separately. The total power consumption of the VBS (P) will be the summation of power consumed by BBU and RRU, which is defined in equation [5.10]:

$$P = P_B + P_R \qquad\qquad [5.10]$$

where P_B represents the power consumption of the BBU and P_R denotes the power consumption of the RRU in the VBS. The intermediate result of the EARTH model [AUE 11, ZHA 14] defines the RRU power consumption according to equation [5.11]:

$$P_R = \frac{P_{out}}{\eta} + P_{RF} \qquad\qquad [5.11]$$

where η represents the efficiency of power amplifier (PA) and P_{RF} represents the power consumption of radio circuits.

The central processing unit (CPU) is the main element in the BBU processing, and hence it consumes a large amount of power to execute required instructions. The main memory also consumes a considerable amount of power, which can be ignored, because it is directly connected to the CPU. The energy consumption in the BBU [ZHA 14] can be calculated with the following equations:

$$P_B = N_c \left(P_{Bmin} + \triangle_{P_B} \tau_c s^{\beta} \right) \qquad [5.12]$$

and

$$\triangle_{P_B} = \left(P_{B_{max}} - P_{B_{min}} \right) / s_0^{\beta} \qquad [5.13]$$

where N_c represents the number of active cores in the CPU. The maximum and minimum power consumption of each core is denoted by P_{Bmax} and P_{Bmin}, respectively; τ_c illustrates the percentage of CPU load on the active cores (N_c), which is generated by the BBU processes; s is the CPU speed; s_0 is the reference of CPU speed (i.e. s and s_0 can be same) and β is the exponential coefficient of CPU speed. The CPU load τ_c is defined as

$$\tau_c = \frac{I(r)}{N_c s} = \frac{c_0 + kr}{N_c s} \qquad [5.14]$$

where $I(r)$ represents the instruction per unit time (which is linear with r), $N_c s$ denotes the processing of maximum instructions per unit time and c_0 and k are coefficients of data transmission rate r. Based on the profiling results of CloudIQ, the total power consumed by BBU [ZHA 14] is calculated as follows:

$$P_B = N_c P_{Bmin} + \triangle_{P_B} c_0 s^{\beta-1} + \triangle_{P_B} krs^{\beta-1}. \qquad [5.15]$$

Now, the total power consumed by a VBS is defined as

$$P_{in} = \begin{cases} P_B + P_R, & 0 < P_{out} \le P_{max} \\ P_{sleep}, & P_{out} = 0. \end{cases} \qquad [5.16]$$

5.6.2. *User equipment*

Despite recent advancement in end-users' smart devices, UEs still struggle with short battery life, which directly affects the user satisfaction level while using different wireless networks. There are various factors of UE that consume more battery power, such as larger screen size, several processor cores, different radio access technologies (e.g. WiFi, EDGE, HSPA, LTE-A) and popular power hungry applications that reduce the operational battery life to few hours.

The 5G communication system is still in its early stage as 3rd Generation Partner Project (3GPP) has not released any standard specification. Similarly, the UE DRX mechanism in 5G mobile communication system is not known yet. In this circumstance, a simple approach can be used to model the overall UE's power consumption [JEN 12, LAU 13], which is defined by equation [5.17]:

$$P_{total} = UE_{con} \times P_{con} + UE_{idle} \times P_{idle} + UE_{DRX} \times P_{DRX} \quad [5.17]$$

where P_{total} is the total power consumption of the UE and the binary variable UE represents the power consumption in different radio resource configuration (RRC) modes (i.e. *connected, idle* and DRX). Similarly, the variables P_{con}, P_{idle} and P_{DRX} represent the power consumption of UE in a specific mode.

The DRX method in LTE-A is a three-step DRX process, which allows us to save more power during the inactive cycle of the UE. In 5G, the 3GPP may introduce intermediate states in existing DRX process of 4G (LTE-A) for reducing the network delay and saving more UE power. The network delay impacts the user-perceived service quality (i.e. QoE), and researchers have included the QoE in network decisions to ensure a high customer satisfaction with minimum network resources [MUS 14b]. The 5G network can configure the UE with different DRX cycles based on network characteristics and user-perceived service experience. The additional/intermediate DRX states might depend on the different traffic models and end-user's device battery requirement. Based on additional intermediate states, we consider DRX models with four and five states for 5G networks in order to optimize the UE's power consumption and reduce network delay. Figure 5.11 shows these additional intermediate active states, S_4 and S_5, which extends the original

LTE-A three-state DRX model (Figure 5.9) to four-state and five-state models, as shown in Figure 5.11(a) and Figure 5.11(b), respectively.

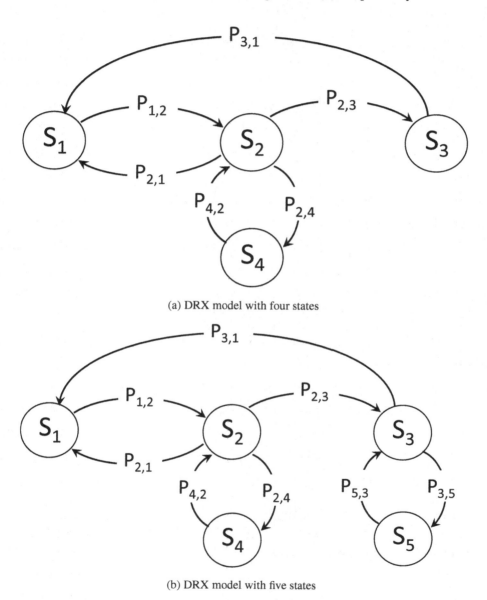

(a) DRX model with four states

(b) DRX model with five states

Figure 5.11. *DRX model with four and five states*

The transitions between new states in the DRX mechanism are defined by the semi-Markov process in order to obtain an embedded Markov chain and get the state transition probabilities p_{ij}, where $i, j \in \{1, 2, 3, 4\}$ and $i, j \in \{1, 2, 3, 4, 5\}$ for four-state and five-state DRX models, respectively. The transition probability matrix for DRX four and five states are given in equations [5.18]–[5.19], respectively:

$$P_{4-state} = \begin{pmatrix} P_{1,1} & P_{1,2} & 0 & 0 \\ P_{2,1} & 0 & P_{2,3} & P_{2,4} \\ 1 & 0 & 0 & 0 \\ 0 & 1 & 0 & 0 \end{pmatrix} \qquad [5.18]$$

$$P_{5-state} = \begin{pmatrix} P_{1,1} & P_{1,2} & 0 & 0 & 0 \\ P_{2,1} & 0 & P_{2,3} & P_{2,4} & 0 \\ P_{3,1} & 0 & 0 & 0 & P_{3,5} \\ 0 & 1 & 0 & 0 & 0 \\ 0 & 0 & 1 & 0 & 0 \end{pmatrix} \qquad [5.19]$$

We leverage the result from previous work [FOW 15] in order to determine the PS factor and wake-up delay ($E[D]$). In the DRX mechanism, the PS factor (in percentage) determines how much power is saved while keeping the UE in sleep mode. The PS factors for four-state and five-state DRX models are expressed as follows:

$$PS_{4-state} = \frac{\pi_2 E[H_2^{eff}] + \pi_3 E[H_3^{eff}]}{\sum_{i=1}^{4} E[H_i]} \qquad [5.20]$$

$$PS_{5-state} = \frac{\pi_2 E[H_2^{eff}] + \pi_3 E[H_3^{eff}]}{\sum_{i=1}^{5} E[H_i]} \qquad [5.21]$$

where π represents the probability of staying at state S_i, $E[H_i]$ denotes the holding time in state S_i (where $i \in 1, 2, 3, 4, 5$) and $E[H_i^{eff}]$ is the effective holding time, which represents instant ON duration during sleep time.

The wake-up delay ($E[D]$) factor for DRX short cycles (DS) and DRX long cycles (DL) is expressed as follows:

$$E[D] = \sum_{i=1}^{N_{DS}} p_i \frac{t_{DS}}{2} + \sum_{i=N_{DS}+1}^{\infty} p_i \frac{t_{DL}}{2} \qquad [5.22]$$

where t_{DS} is a sequence of DRX short cycles during light sleep periods, N_{DS} is the number of DRX short cycles, t_{DL} is the number of deep sleep periods and N_{DS} is the number of DRX long cycles.

5.7. Results

Here, we evaluate the performance of various DRX states of UE and power consumed by the VBS in 5G networks. The performance evaluations are observed in terms of percentage of the PS factor and wake-up delay using the ETSI bursty data traffic model. The main parameters related to the VBS are defined in Table 5.1, and the numerical values used for modeling the traffic data are $\lambda_{ip} = 10$, $\lambda_{is} = \dfrac{1}{2000}$, $\lambda_{ipc} = \dfrac{1}{30}$, $\lambda_p = 10$, $\mu_p = 25$ and $\mu_{pc} = 5$.

CPU speed (s)/ reference speed (s_0)	2 GHz
Maximum power per CPU core (P_{Bmax})	20 W
Minimum power per CPU core (P_{Bmin})	5 W
Constant coefficient of instruction speed ($c0$)	7×10^8
Rate-varying coefficient of instruction (k)	35
RF circuit power (P_{RF})	12.9
Power amplifier efficiency (η)	31.1%
VBS sleeping power (P_{sleep})	6.45 W

Table 5.1. *Important VBS parameters*

Figure 5.12 shows the performance of various DRX state models in terms of Inactivity Timer t_I. The increasing values of t_I hold the UE in an active state for a longer period which consumes more power, as shown in Figure 5.12(a). Similarly, longer active states also reduce the delay time because the UE listens to the VBS to download the required schedule data, and the decreasing trends of delay are plotted against the increasing values of t_I in Figure 5.12(b).

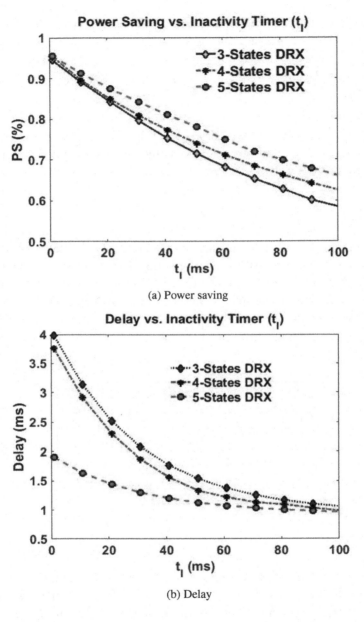

(a) Power saving

(b) Delay

Figure 5.12. *Impact of inactivity timer t_I. For a color version of the figure, see www.iste.co.uk/mushtaq/systems.zip*

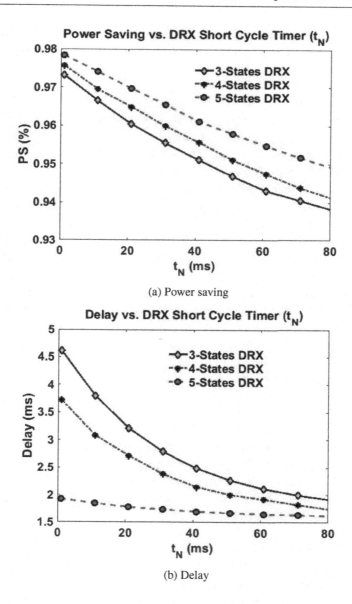

(a) Power saving

(b) Delay

Figure 5.13. *Impact of DRX short cycle timer t_N. For a color version of the figure, see www.iste.co.uk/mushtaq/systems.zip*

The impact of DRX short cycle timer t_N in terms of PS and delay is illustrated in Figure 5.13. The results show that by increasing t_N values, the four-state DRX model outperforms the three-state DRX model, while the five-state DRX model shows better performance in terms of both PS and delay.

There are two possible scenarios for the VBS: (1) if the UE is in sleep mode, then the BS might use the available computational resources to serve other UEs in the empty time slot and (2) the VBS will move into sleep mode to save power. In our case, we take into account the second scenario; when a UE is in sleep mode, the BS will also move into sleep mode and consume less power (i.e. $6.45W$). Figure 5.14 consists of two y-axes, where the left y-axis represents the power consumed by UE (mW) and the right y-axis represents the power consumed by the VBS with respect to the impact of t_I and t_N on UE and VBS in different DRX states. In general, there is a DRX manager in the BS, which keeps track of the DRX status of the UE and contributes in the packet-scheduling decision for UE [MUS 16]. The DRX manager in the VBS closely coordinates the DRX status of UE, which causes the VBS to consume less power because UE is in the sleeping state, as shown in Figure 5.14. When the duration of inactivity timer (t_I) increases as shown in Figure 5.14(a), UE spends more time in an active state, thereby consuming more power after it is powered ON and monitoring the PDCCH from the VBS which is also in power consumption mode to serve the UE.

Figure 5.14(b) shows the impact of t_N on UE and VBS by increasing the values of t_N. It should be noted that by increasing the values of t_N, the UE spends more time in Light Sleep mode (consumes less power), but wakes up frequently to listen to the PDCCH from the VBS (consumes less power). Increase in t_N values reduces the power saving [FOW 13] (see Figure 5.13(a)) and consumes more power as shown in Figure 5.14(b), but it also reduces the delay (see Figure 5.13(b)).

The results in Figure 5.15 depict the impact of DRX short cycle (t_{DS}) on PS and delay. It can be observed that by increasing the values of t_{DS}, the PS in all DRX models starts increasing as opposite to t_I and t_N, because the UE switches to a very short OFF period (sleep mode) and a very small ON duration (listening to PDCCH). The results from Figure 5.15 show that PS improved in both the four-state and five-state DRX models compared with the three-state DRX model. Similarly, delay also reduces in the four-state and five-state DRX models against the three-state DRX model, as shown in Figure 5.15.

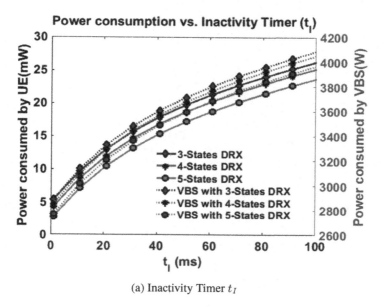

(a) Inactivity Timer t_I

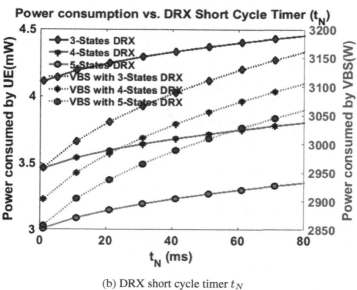

(b) DRX short cycle timer t_N

Figure 5.14. *Impact of t_I & t_N on UE and VBS. For a color version of the figure, see www.iste.co.uk/mushtaq/systems.zip*

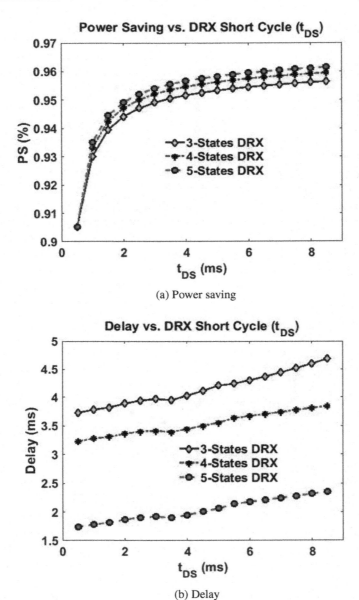

(a) Power saving

(b) Delay

Figure 5.15. *Impact of DRX short cycle t_{DS}. For a color version of the figure, see www.iste.co.uk/mushtaq/systems.zip*

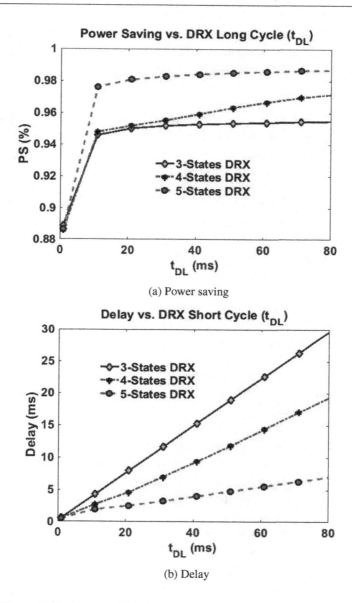

(a) Power saving

(b) Delay

Figure 5.16. *Impact of DRX long cycle t_{DL}. For a color version of the figure, see www.iste.co.uk/mushtaq/systems.zip*

Figure 5.16 shows the performance of four-state and five-state DRX models compared with the three-state DRX model in terms of t_{DL}. The results show improvement in the four-state DRX model and even greater improvement in the five-state DRX model compared with the three-state DRX model in terms of both PS and delay. By increasing the value of t_{DL}, the UE not only spends more time in sleep mode, but also increases the delay, as shown in Figure 5.16.

Figure 5.17 shows the impact of t_{DS} and t_{DL} on UE and VBS. The results clearly show that the VBS considers the DRX state of the UE and switches between power-saving mode and sleeping mode based on the UE DRX state. It can be observed that power consumption reduces in the case of t_{DS} and t_{DL} when compared with power consumption increase in the case of t_I and t_N (see Figure 5.14). Figure 5.17(a) shows that the four-state DRX model utilizes less power than the three-state DRX model, while the five-state DRX model utilizes less power than the four-state DRX model in both UE and VBS power consumption. The same pattern of less power utilization is illustrated in Figure 5.17(b) for all three DRX states. However, it can be observed that when t_{DL} value increases, UE stays in Deep Light mode (no power utilization) and saves more UE power by linearly decreasing the power consumption, as shown in Figure 5.17(b). On the contrary, the VBS consumes less power as it spends more time in the sleeping state.

This chapter addressed two key aspects of 5G network in terms of QoE and power-saving model. In the case of QoE, it described a method that minimized the overall network delay of both multimedia services, i.e. the CBR (VoIP) and VBR (video streaming) traffic models. The impact of network delay on user satisfaction was measured by the proposed QoE method to calculate the user's QoE for video streaming services, and the performance of this method was compared with the QoV method. The results showed that the proposed analytical method was successfull in reducing the overall network delay, which was less than 1 ms. They also showed that the low delay significantly improved the user's QoE. The performance of the proposed QoE method was evaluated by considering the impact of delay and PLR on user-perceived QoE for video streaming services. The proposed QoE method outperfomed the QoV method in terms of delay and PLR.

The VoIP traffic is a delay-sensitive service, and our proposed method effectively reduced the network delay. The standard methods proposed in the literature are unable to calculate the user's QoE for VoIP because of very low delay. In this context, based on our proposed analytical method, we can state that the user's QoE will be maximum for a very low delay. In future work, we will propose a QoE measurement method for VoIP in 5G networks that will also consider energy saving in mobile devices.

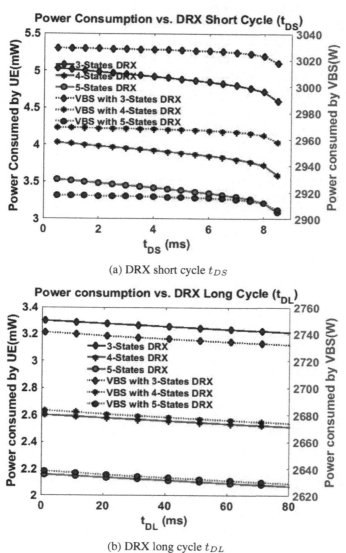

(a) DRX short cycle t_{DS}

(b) DRX long cycle t_{DL}

Figure 5.17. *Impact of t_{DS} & t_{DL} on UE and VBS. For a color version of the figure, see www.iste.co.uk/mushtaq/systems.zip*

From the perspective of the power-saving model, this chapter presented a new power-saving model for mobile devices and the VBS in 5G cellular networks. The proposed method used the component-based strategy to calculate power consumption based on different elements in the VBS and DRX states of the UE. An extended DRX state of the LTE-A network was developed by adding the additional DRX states in the original three-state DRX model of LTE-A. However, the power consumption model of the VBS used different elements of RRH and BBU in order to calculate the total power consumed by the VBS. It can be observed that more power was saved by using the additional DRX states (four-state and five-state DRX models) together with the original three-state DRX model of LTE-A; moreover, the additional states reduced the delay. In future work, the proposed method will be evaluated using different traffic models, and the impact of various DRX timers will be evaluated for different traffic models in order to optimize the DRX mechanism of 5G networks.

Conclusion

Communication systems are always evolving and trying to fulfill the increasing traffic demands, providing good QoS to achieve high user satisfaction. The concept of QoE comprises both technical and non-technical perspectives that directly/indirectly influence the user perception, while QoS represents the network's ability to provide service only from a technical perspective. Hence, QoE and QoS are different but interdependent. This is because QoS is a key factor having a high impact on user perception. It is important to consider the QoS in order to study the QoE of different service types. From the perspective of QoE, service integrity can be defined in terms of QoS parameters such as jitter, delay, packet loss rate and throughput. The accurate measurement of QoE, which is influenced by distinct QoS parameters, is not an easy task; however, it is necessary to develop an optimal method that considers the QoS for the best network performance and achieves high user satisfaction.

In this book, we described different methods to investigate a user's QoE from the viewpoint of technical and non-technical parameters using multimedia services (video and VoIP). We discussed two approaches for collecting datasets to assess the QoE of video services. The "subjective" dataset helps analyze the user's profiles and sheds light on key factors to help network service providers understand end-users' behavior and expectations. This dataset highlights the role of variable video qualities based on QoS parameters in influencing the user perception. This motivates us to develop an adaptive video streaming method that will help change the video quality based on the network's state and the user device's properties. In future communication networks, resources and power optimization will be key challenges because multimedia services are resource and power hungry. In this context, we also presented a scheduling method to allocate resources to the end-user based on the user's QoE and optimize the power efficiency of the user's device for LTE-A.

Book summary

The objective of this book was to investigate the concept of QoE for multimedia services by analyzing technical and non-technical parameters, and quantify the performance of offered services as well as their impact on end-users. The book can be summarized as follows:

1) Two subjective methods that were used to collect datasets for assessing QoE of video services and to analyze the impact of several parameters were presented. These methods were based on controlled and uncontrolled environmental approaches. In the controlled approach, a testbed experiment was set up to measure the influence of different parameters on user-perceived QoE while watching the video service. The impact of different parameters (QoS parameters, video characteristics, device types, etc.) on user perception was recorded in the form of a MOS. The "subjective" dataset was used to investigate the correlation between QoS and QoE. Six ML classifiers were used to classify the collected dataset. The results indicated that among the classifiers, decision tree (DT) showed good performance in terms of the mean absolute error rate. An instance classification test was also carried out to select the best model, and the results showed that both RF and DT performed approximately at the same level. Finally, to evaluate the efficiency of DT and RF, a statistical analysis of classification was performed, and the results showed that RF performed slightly better than DT.

2) The datasets were also used to investigate the impact of different QoS parameters on users' profiles, and the comprehensive study of users' profiles gave useful information to network service providers in order to understand the behavior and expectations of end-users. The analysis showed that viewers of interesting video content were more tolerant than those of non-interesting video content. Similarly, users of HD video content were more sensitive to delay and packet loss rates, while those of non-HD video content had more tolerant levels. Based on the analysis of users' profiles, network service providers can efficiently manage their resources to improve user satisfaction.

3) In the uncontrolled environment, a crowdsourcing application tool to investigate the users' QoE in real time was developed. The application tool used a feedback form to subjectively record the user perception. It monitored and stored the performance of real-time QoS parameters (packet loss, delay, jitter and throughput). In addition, the tool also measureed the real-time performance characteristics of the end-user's device in terms of system memory, performance capacity, CPU usage and other parameters.

4) Important adaptive video streaming technologies that run on unmanaged networks to achieve certain QoS features were presented. These adaptive video streaming technologies were developed by well-known organizations such as Adobe, Microsoft, Apple and MPEG. HTTP adaptive streaming technologies provided by popular companies, such as Adobe's HDS, Apple's HLS, Microsoft's MSS and MPEG's DASH, were discussed briefly.

5) The client-side HTTP rate-adaptive BBF method that was used to adapt the video quality based on three main QoS parameters, namely dynamic network bandwidth, user's buffer status and dropped frame rate, was proposed. The BBF method was evaluated using different buffer lengths. The results showed that a greater buffer length was less affected by dynamic bandwidth, but the network resources were also not efficiently utilized. The BBF method was evaluated and compared with Adobe's OSMF streaming method. The result showed that BBF was successful in managing situations compared with OSMF in terms of sudden decreases in bandwidth and dropped frame rates when the client system did not have enough resources to decode the frames. In addition, the BBF method optimized the user's QoE by avoiding stalling and pausing during video playback.

6) The downlink scheduling algorithm QEPEM was proposed for delay-sensitive traffic (VoIP). The QEPEM tried to enhance the QoE and provided better QoS by decreasing packet losses, improving fairness between UE and considering the QoS requirement of multimedia services. It could assure QoS in the power-saving environment of high user satisfaction. The QEPEM maximized the user's QoE by using user perception in its scheduling decision. Furthermore, its performance was compared with traditional schemes based on different QoS attributes using simulations. The result showed that the packet loss rate had a higher influence on QoE than delay. The QEPEM was evaluated in the power-saving mode, and the impact of power saving on QoS and QoE was also examined. In the power-saving environment, the QEPEM performed remarkably better than traditional schemes with better user experience because it allocated resources efficiently and fairly between UE.

7) Two key aspects of 5G networks in terms of QoE and the power-saving model were addressed. An analytical method to minimize the overall network delay of multimedia services, such as CBR (VoIP) and VBR (video streaming) traffic models, was discussed. The impact of network delay on user satisfaction was measured by the proposed QoE method. This method calculated the user's QoE of video streaming services. The performance of the proposed QoE method was evaluated by considering the impact of delay and PLR on user-perceived QoE of video streaming services. From the power-saving model's perspective, a new power-saving model was proposed for mobile devices and VBS in 5G cellular networks. The proposed method used the component-based strategy to calculate power consumption based on different elements in VBS and DRX states of the UE. An extended DRX state of the LTE-A network was developed by adding additional DRX states in the original three-state DRX model of LTE-A. However, VBS's power consumption model used different elements of RRH and BBU in order to calculate the total power consumed by a VBS. It can be observed that more power was saved by adding additional DRX states (four-state DRX and five-state DRX) in the original three-state DRX model of LTE-A; moreover, these additional states reduced the delay.

Future perspectives

This book addressed the challenges of investigating users' QoE of multimedia services and highlighted the impacts of different parameters on user perception. Several future research directions and open issues can be deduced from our work and summarized as follows:

1) Analyzing users' profiles under different scenarios can provide key information to network service providers that will help them to understand the user's behavior and expectations. We will analyze the influence exerted on the user's profile by different factors and parameters, e.g. terminal types (HD TV, 10 inch tablets, smart mobile device and LCD screen), while traveling (car, bus, train, etc.), and we will also apply statistical analysis techniques.

2) Crowdsourcing is considered as a key technique to evaluate and measure service quality in a real environment in which a user expresses his/her perceived quality. We will extend the functionality of our proposed crowdsourcing application tool by adding it to the Firefox extension and Java application. It will help to analyze the impact of other parameters on the user's QoE in the real-time environment.

3) The Internet is a collection of diverse networks with different access techniques, which has forced network service providers to develop a solution for unpredictable network characteristics. The rate-adaptive video streaming method is developed to solve the problem by considering different parameters at the client side. In this context, we proposed the HTTP-based rate-adaptive video streaming method BBF to adapt video quality by considering three important QoS parameters, namely bandwidth, buffer and dropped frame rate, observed at the client side. In the future, we will extend the proposed BBF method to optimize its performance by measuring the real-time user's QoE and select the appropriate video quality based on user-perceived QoE. A complete adaptive streaming model will be developed and evaluated.

4) The power-saving method has a direct influence on the QoS of multimedia services because more power saving will increase the packet delays that may result in packet loss and low user-perceived QoE. To overcome this problem, we will optimize the DRX parameters to maximize the user perception as well as power saving without imposing more packet delays. The proposed QEPEM will be evaluated with other traffic models, e.g. video, ftp, gaming, and the impact of these traffic models along with the power-saving mechanism on user satisfaction will be measured. The effects of UE handover on eNodeB in terms of mobility will also be observed and we will extend QEPEM for future mobile communication networks because user perception and efficient power utilization are key challenges in NGN.

5) 5G will bring new innovations in cellular networks, as well as create new challenges, which need to be addressed effectively to improve user satisfaction and thus achieve the business goal of network operators. The real-time prediction of user's QoE and optimization of power both at UE and VBS are key elements of 5G networks. We will develop QoE prediction methods for different traffic models (e.g. VoIP), which will also consider energy saving of the mobile device based on the performance of 5G network elements. Similarly, the impact of various DRX timers should be optimized for various traffic models in order to optimize the DRX mechanism of 5G networks.

Bibliography

[3GP 05] 3GPP, User Equipment (UE) procedures in idle mode and procedures for cell reselection in connected mode, Technical Specification, TS 25.304 version 5.9.0 Release 5, 2005.

[3GP 07] 3GPP, LTE physical layer framework for performance verification radio access network (RAN), TSG-RAN1 no.48, R1-070674, 2007.

[ADO 10] ADOBE MEDIA SERVER DEVELOPER, Recommendation, Video Endcoding for HTTP Dynamic Streaming on Flash Platform, Adobe Media Server Developer, 2010.

[ADO 16] ADOBE, "Overview of HTTP Dynamic Streaming and HTTP Live Streaming", available at: https://helpx.adobe.com/adobe-media-server/dev/configure-dynamic-streaming-live-streaming.html, 2016.

[AGB 08] AGBOMA F., LIOTTA A., "QoE-aware QoS Management", *Proceedings of the 6th International Conference on Advances in Mobile Computing and Multimedia*, MoMM '08, ACM, pp. 111–116, 2008.

[AHO 09] AHO K., REPO I., NIHTILA T. *et al.*, "Analysis of VoIP over HSDPA performance with discontinuous reception cycles", *6th International Conference on Information Technology: New Generations*, pp. 1190–1194, April 2009.

[AHO 11] AHO K., HENTTONEN T., PUTTONEN J. *et al.*, "User equipment energy efficiency versus LTE network performance", *International Journal on Advances in Telecommunications*, vol. 3, no. 4, pp. 27–38, 2011.

[AKH 12] AKHSHABI S., ANANTAKRISHNAN L., BEGEN A. C. *et al.*, "What happens when HTTP adaptive streaming players compete for bandwidth?", *Proceedings of the 22nd International Workshop on Network and Operating System Support for Digital Audio and Video*, pp. 9–14, 2012.

[ANA 09] ANANTHANARAYANAN G., STOICA I., "Blue-Fi: enhancing Wi-Fi performance using bluetooth signals", *Proceedings of the 7th International Conference on Mobile Systems, Applications, and Services*, MobiSys'09, ACM, New York, USA, pp. 249–262, 2009.

[APP 17] APPLE, "HTTP Live Streaming Overview", available at: https://developer.apple.com/streaming/, 2017.

[ARA 14] ARAI S., FADLULLAH Z.M., NGO T. *et al.*, "An efficient method for minimizing energy consumption of user equipment in storage-embedded heterogeneous networks", *IEEE Wireless Communications*, vol. 21, no. 4, pp. 70–76, 2014.

[ARO 12] AROUSSI S., BOUABANA-TEBIBEL T., MELLOUK A., "Empirical QoE/QoS correlation model based on multiple parameters for VoD flows", *IEEE Global Communications Conference (GLOBECOM)*, pp. 1963–1968, December 2012.

[AUE 11] AUER G., GIANNINI V., DESSET C. *et al.*, "How much energy is needed to run a wireless network?", *IEEE Wireless Communications*, vol. 18, no. 5, pp. 40–49, 2011.

[AUN 09] AUNG W.T., HLA K.H.M.S., "Random forest classifier for multi-category classification of web pages", *IEEE Asia-Pacific Services Computing Conference, 2009*, pp. 372–376, December 2009.

[BAL 09] BALASUBRAMANIAN N., BALASUBRAMANIAN A., VENKATARAMANI A., "Energy consumption in mobile phones: a measurement study and implications for network applications", *Proceedings of SIGCOMM Conference on Internet Measurement*, pp. 280–293, 2009.

[BEG 11] BEGEN A., AKGUL T., BAUGHER M., "Watching video over the web: Part 1: streaming protocols", *IEEE Internet Computing*, vol. 15, no. 2, pp. 54–63, 2011.

[BEH 08] BEH K. C., ARMOUR S., DOUFEXI A., "Joint Time-frequency domain proportional fair scheduler with HARQ for 3GPP LTE systems", in *IEEE 68th Vehicular Technology Conference*, pp. 1–5, September 2008.

[BO 10] BO H., HUI T., LAN C. *et al.*, "DRX-aware scheduling method for Delay-sensitive traffic", *IEEE Communications Letters*, vol. 14, no. 12, pp. 1113–1115, December 2010.

[BOC 13] BOCHAROV J., ISS Smooth Streaming Transport Protocol, Microsoft, available at: http://www.iis.net/learn/media/smooth-streaming, November 2013.

[BUL 01] BULTERMAN D., "SMIL 2.0 part 1: overview, concepts, and structure", *IEEE MultiMedia*, vol. 8, pp. 82–88, October 2001.

[CAI 14] CAI Y., YU F., BU S., "Cloud computing meets mobile wireless communications in next generation cellular networks", *IEEE Network*, vol. 28, no. 6, pp. 54–59, 2014.

[CAR 10a] CARROLL A., HEISER G., "An analysis of power consumption in a smartphone", *USENIX Annual Technical Conference, ser. USENIXATC 10*, pp. 271–284, June 2010.

[CAR 10b] CARBONE M., RIZZO L., "Dummynet Revisited", *ACM SIGCOMM Computer Communication Review*, vol. 40, no. 2, pp. 12–20, 2010.

[CHE 09] CHEN J., HUANG K., WANG F. *et al.*, "E-learning behavior analysis based on fuzzy clustering", *3rd International Conference on Genetic and Evolutionary Computing*, pp. 863–866, 2009.

[CHE 10] CHEN K.-T., CHANG C.-J., WU C.-C. *et al.*, "Quadrant of euphoria: a crowdsourcing platform for QoE assessment", *IEEE Network*, vol. 24, no. 2, pp. 28–35, 2010.

[CHO 12] CHOI J., KIM M.-G., JEONG H. *et al.*, "Power-saving mechanisms for energy efficient IEEE 802.16e/m", *Journal of Network and Computer Applications*, vol. 35, no. 6, pp. 1728–1739, 2012.

[CIS 13] CISCO SYSTEMS, INC., Cisco Visual Networking Index: Forecast and Methodology, 2013–2017, Cisco Systems, Inc., 2013.

[CIS 16] CISCO SYSTEMS, INC., Cisco Visual Networking Index: Global Mobile Data Traffic Forecast Update 2015–2020, Cisco Systems, Inc., 2016.

[CLA 05] CLAUSSEN H., "Efficient modelling of channel maps with correlated shadow fading in mobile radio systems", *IEEE 16th International Symposium on Personal, Indoor and Mobile Radio Communications*, vol. 1, pp. 512–516, 2005.

[COL 01] COLE R.G., ROSENBLUTH J.H., "Voice over IP performance monitoring", *SIGCOMM Computer Communication*, vol. 31, no. 2, pp. 9–24, 2001.

[COR 10] CORNUEJOLS A., MICLET L., KODRATOFF Y., *Apprentissage artificiel – Concepts et algorithmes*, Eyrolles, Paris, 2010.

[DEC 13] DE CICCO L., CALDARALO V., PALMISANO V. *et al.*, "ELASTIC: a client-side controller for dynamic adaptive streaming over HTTP (DASH)", *20th International Packet Video Workshop (PV)*, pp. 1–8, December 2013.

[DEC 14a] DE CICCO L., COFANO G., MASCOLO S., "A hybrid model of the Akamai adaptive streaming control system", *IFAC World Congress*, August 2014.

[DEC 14b] DE CICCO L., MASCOLO S., "An adaptive video streaming control system: modeling, validation, and performance evaluation", *IEEE/ACM Transactions on Networking*, vol. 22, no. 2, pp. 526–539, 2014.

[DEL 10] DELGADO O., JAUMARD B., "Joint admission control and resource allocation with GoS and QoS in LTE uplink", *IEEE GLOBECOM Workshops (GC Wkshps)*, pp. 829–833, December 2010.

[DIN 03] DING L., GOUBRAN R., "Speech quality prediction in VoIP using the extended E-model", *IEEE Global Telecommunications Conference*, vol. 7, pp. 3974–3978, 2003.

[DON 10] DONTHI S., MEHTA N., "Performance analysis of subband-level channel quality indicator feedback scheme of LTE", *National Conference on Communications*, pp. 1–5, January 2010.

[EDU 11] EDUARDO C., SHERALI Z., MIKOAJ L. *et al.*, "Recent advances in multimedia networking", *Multimedia Tools and Applications*, vol. 54, no. 3, 2011.

[ETS 02] ETSI, Quality of Service (QoS) measurement methodologies. Annex E, method for determining an equipment impairment factor using passive monitoring, TS101 329-5, 2002.

[ETS 07] ETSI, 3GPP; DRX Parameters in LTE; TSG RAN WG2 LTE Contribution, TS 36.300, N. R2-071285, 2007.

[ETS 10] ETSI, Technical specification group radio access network evolved universal terrestial radio access physical layer procedures, TS 36.213 V9.3.0, 2010.

[ETS 11a] ETSI, LTE RAN enhancements for diverse data applications – 3GPP, RAN Plenary Contribution, RP-110410, 2011.

[ETS 11b] ETSI, Medium access control protocol specification, TS 36.321 version 10.2.0 Release 10, 2011.

[ETS 12] ETSI, Evolved universal terrestrial radio access (E-UTRA), radio resource control (RRC), TS 36.331 version 11.0.0 Release 11, 2012.

[FAN 08] FAN Y., LUNDEN P., KUUSELA M. *et al.*, "Efficient Semi-persistent scheduling for VoIP on EUTRA downlink", *IEEE 68th Vehicular Technology Conference*, pp. 1–5, September 2008.

[FAR 12] FARKAS V., HEDER B., NOVACZKI S., "A split connection TCP proxy in LTE networks", *18th European Conference on Information and Communication Technologies – Lecture Notes in Computer Science*, pp. 263–274, 2012.

[FEH 11] FEHSKE A., FETTWEIS G., MALMODIN J. *et al.*, "The global footprint of mobile communications: the ecological and economic perspective", *IEEE Communications Magazine*, vol. 49, no. 8, pp. 55–62, August 2011.

[FIE 10] FIEDLER M., HOSSFELD T., TRAN-GIA P., "A generic quantitative relationship between quality of experience and quality of service", *IEEE Network*, vol. 24, no. 2, pp. 36–41, 2010.

[FOW 11] FOWLER S., "Study on power saving based on radio frame in LTE wireless communication system using DRX", *IEEE Globecom Joint Workshop of SCPA and SaCoNAS*, December 2011.

[FOW 12] FOWLER S., BHAMBER R.S., MELLOUK A., "Analysis of adjustable and fixed DRX mechanism for power saving in LTE/LTE-Advanced," *IEEE International Conference on Communications*, Ottawa, ON, pp. 1964–1969, 2012.

[FOW 13] FOWLER S., MELLOUK A., YAMADA N., *LTE-Advanced DRX Mechanism for Power Saving*, ISTE Ltd, London and John Wiley & Sons, New York, 2013.

[FOW 15] FOWLER S., SHAHIDULLAH A., OSMAN M. *et al.*, "Analytical evaluation of extended DRX with additional active cycles for light traffic", *Computer Network*, vol. 77, no. C, pp. 90–102, 2015.

[FRE 11] FRENCH H., LIN J., PHAN T. *et al.*, "Real time video QoE analysis of RTMP streams", *Performance Computing and Communications Conference (IPCCC), IEEE 30th International*, pp. 1–2, November 2011.

[GAR 12] GARDLO B., RIES M., HOSSFELD T. *et al.*, "Microworkers vs. Facebook: the impact of crowdsourcing platform choice on experimental results", *Fourth International Workshop on Quality of Multimedia Experience*, pp. 35–36, 2012.

[HAN 09] HAN Y.-T., KIM M.-G., PARK H.-S., "A novel server selection method to achieve delay-based fairness in the server palm", *IEEE Communications Letters*, vol. 13, no. 11, pp. 868–870, November 2009.

[HOS 11a] HOSFELD T., BIEDERMANN S., SCHATZ R. *et al.*, "The memory effect and its implications on web QoE modeling", *23rd International Teletraffic Congress*, pp. 103–110, September 2011.

[HOS 11b] HOSSFELD T., SEUFERT M., HIRTH M. *et al.*, "Quantification of YouTube QoE via Crowdsourcing", *IEEE International Symposium on Multimedia*, pp. 494–499, 2011.

[HUA 12] HUANG T.-Y., HANDIGOL N., HELLER B. *et al.*, "Confused, timid, and unstable: picking a video streaming rate is hard", *Proceedings of the ACM Conference on Internet Measurement Conference*, pp. 225–238, 2012.

[HUA 14a] HUAWEI, 5G, A Technology Vision, Huawei White Paper, available at: http://www.huawei.com/5gwhitepaper/, 2014.

[HUA 14b] HUANG T.-Y., JOHARI R., MCKEOWN N. *et al.*, "A buffer-based approach to rate adaptation: evidence from a large video streaming service", *Proceedings of the ACM Conference on SIGCOMM*, ACM, New York, USA, pp. 187–198, August 2014.

[HUA 14c] HUANG T.-Y., JOHARI R., MCKEOWN N. *et al.*, "Using the buffer to avoid rebuffers: evidence from a large video streaming service", *arXiv:1401.2209*, January 2014.

[IKU 10] IKUNO J.C., WRULICH M., RUPP M., "System level simulation of LTE networks", *IEEE 71st Vehicular Technology Conference*, Taipei, Taiwan, pp. 1–5, May 2010.

[INT 96] INTERNATIONAL TELECOMMUNICATION UNION, Methods for subjective determination of transmission quality, ITU-T Recommendation P.800, 1996.

[INT 97] INTERNATIONAL TELECOMMUNICATION UNION, M.1225: Guidelines for evaluation of radio transmission technologies for IMT-2000, ITU-R Recommendation M.1225, 1997.

[INT 01a] INTERNATIONAL TELECOMMUNICATION UNION, Speech codecs. Evaluation of speech quality (PESQ): an objective method for end-to-end speech quality assessment of narrow-band telephone networks, ITU-T Recommendation P.862, 2001.

[INT 01b] INTERNATIONAL TELECOMMUNICATION UNION, Methodology for derivation of equipment impairment factors from subjective listening-only tests, ITU-T Recommendation P.833, 2001.

[INT 07a] INTERNATIONAL TELECOMMUNICATION UNION, Definition of quality of experience. Appendix I, ITU-T Recommendation P.10/G.100, 2007.

[INT 07b] INTERNATIONAL TELECOMMUNICATION UNION, Transmission impairments due to speech processing, ITU-T Recommendation G.113, November 2007.

[INT 08] INTERNATIONAL TELECOMMUNICATION UNION, Subjective video quality assessment methods for multimedia applications, ITU-T Recommendation P.910, 2008.

[INT 09] INTERNATIONAL TELECOMMUNICATION UNION, Methodology for the subjective assessment of the quality of television pictures, ITU-R Recommendation BT.500-12, 2009.

[INT 11] INTERNATIONAL TELECOMMUNICATION UNION, The E model: a computational model for use in transmission planning, ITU-T Recommendation G.107, 2011.

[ISL 07] ISLAM M., WU Q., AHMADI M. *et al.*, "Investigating the performance of Naive-Bayes classifiers and K-Nearest neighbor classifiers", *International Conference on Convergence Information Technology*, pp. 1541–1546, 2007.

[ISO 13] ISO, IEC 23009-1:2012, Part 1: Media presentation description and segment formats, 2013.

[JAI 91] JAIN R., *The Art of Computer Systems Performance Analysis: Techniques for Experimental Design, Measurement, Simulation and Modeling*, John Wiley & Sons, New York, 1991.

[JAN 10] JANOWSKI L., ROMANIAK P., "QoE as a function of frame rate and resolution changes", *Proceedings of the Third international conference on Future Multimedia Networking*, pp. 34–45, 2010.

[JAR 11] JARSCHEL M., SCHLOSSER D., SCHEURING S. *et al.*, "An evaluation of QoE in cloud gaming based on subjective tests", *Proceedings of the 2011 Fifth International Conference on Innovative Mobile and Internet Services in Ubiquitous Computing*, Washington, DC, pp. 330–335, 2011.

[JEN 12] JENSEN A.R., LAURIDSEN M., MOGENSEN P. *et al.*, "LTE UE power consumption model: for system level energy and performance optimization", *IEEE Vehicular Technology Conference*, pp. 1–5, September 2012.

[JHA 12] JHA S., KOÇ A., VANNITHAMBY R., "Optimization of discontinuous reception (DRX) for mobile internet applications over LTE", in *IEEE Vehicular Technology Conference*, September 2012.

[JIA 12] JIAN W., YIQUN W., SHENG Z. *et al.*, "Traffic-aware power adaptation and base station sleep control for energy-delay tradeoffs in green cellular networks", *IEEE Global Communications Conference*, pp. 3171–3176, December 2012.

[JIA 14] JIANG J., SEKAR V., ZHANG H., "Improving fairness, efficiency, and stability in HTTP-based adaptive video streaming with festive", *IEEE/ACM Transactions on Networking*, vol. 22, pp. 326–340, February 2014.

[JIN 12] JIN S., QIAO D., "Numerical analysis of the power saving in 3GPP LTE advanced wireless metworks", *IEEE Transactions on Vehicular Technology*, vol. 61, no. 4, pp. 1779–1785, 2012.

[JUR 11] JURGELIONIS A., LAULAJAINEN J., HIRVONEN M. *et al.*, "An empirical study of NetEm network emulation functionalities", *Proceedings of 20th International Conference on Computer Communications and Networks*, pp. 1–6, 2011.

[KIM 08] KIM H.J., LEE D.H., LEE J.M. *et al.*, "The QoE evaluation method through the QoS-QoE correlation model", *Fourth International Conference on Networked Computing and Advanced Information Management*, vol. 2, pp. 719–725, September 2008.

[KIM 12] KIM H.J., YUN D.G., KIM H.-S. *et al.*, "QoE assessment model for video streaming service using QoS parameters in wired-wireless network", *14th International Conference on Advanced Communication Technology*, pp. 459–464, 2012.

[KLE 75] KLEINROCK L., *Theory, Volume 1, Queueing Systems*, Wiley-Interscience, Hoboken, 1975.

[KRA 03] KRASIC C., WALPOLE J., FENG W.-C., "Quality-adaptive media streaming by priority drop", *Proceedings of the 13th International Workshop on Network and Operating Systems Support for Digital Audio and Video*, ACM, pp. 112–121, 2003.

[KRI 11] KRISHNAPPA D., KHEMMARAT S., ZINK M., "Planet YouTube: global, measurement-based performance analysis of viewer's experience watching user generated videos", *IEEE 36th Conference on Local Computer Networks*, pp. 948–956, 2011.

[KUS 10] KUSCHNIG R., KOFLER I., HELLWAGNER H., "An evaluation of TCP-based rate-control algorithms for adaptive internet streaming of H.264/SVC", *Proceedings of the 1st Annual ACM SIGMM Conference on Multimedia Systems*, ACM, pp. 157–168, 2010.

[LAM 04] LAM L. S., LEE J., LIEW S. *et al.*, "A transparent rate adaptation algorithm for streaming video over the Internet", *18th International Conference on Advanced Information Networking and Applications*, vol. 1, pp. 346–351, 2004.

[LAU 13] LAURIDSEN M., MOGENSEN P., NOEL L., "Empirical LTE smartphone power model with DRX operation for system level simulations", *IEEE Vehicular Technology Conference*, pp. 1–6, September 2013.

[LAU 14] LAURIDSEN M., NOEL L., SRENSEN T.B. *et al.*, "An empirical LTE smartphone power model with a view to energy efficiency evolution", *Technology Journal*, vol. 8, no. 1, pp. 172–193, 2014.

[LED 12] LEDERER S., MÜLLER C., TIMMERER C., "Dynamic adaptive streaming over HTTP dataset", *Proceedings of the 3rd Multimedia Systems Conference*, ACM, New York, pp. 89–94, 2012.

[LI 14] LI Z., ZHU X., GAHM J. *et al.*, "Probe and adapt: rate adaptation for HTTP video streaming at scale", *IEEE Journal on Selected Areas in Communications*, vol. 32, no. 4, pp. 719–733, 2014.

[LIN 08] LIN Y., YUE G., "Channel-adapted and buffer-aware packet scheduling in LTE wireless communication system", *4th International Conference on Wireless Communications, Networking and Mobile Computing*, pp. 1–4, October 2008.

[LIN 16] LINUX FOUNDATION WIKI, NetEM, available at: http://www.linuxfoundation.org/collaborate/workgroups/networking/netem, 2016.

[LIU 11] LIU C., BOUAZIZI I., GABBOUJ M., "Rate adaptation for adaptive HTTP streaming", *Proceedings of the 2nd Annual ACM Conference on Multimedia Systems*, pp. 169–174, 2011.

[LU 11] LU Z., YANG Y., WEN X. *et al.*, "A cross-layer resource allocation scheme for ICIC in LTE-advanced", *Journal of Network and Computer Applications, Elsevier*, vol. 34, no. 6, pp. 1861–1868, 2011.

[MCC 04] MCCARTHY J.D., SASSE M.A., MIRAS D., "Sharp or smooth?: comparing the effects of quantization vs. frame rate for streamed video", *Proceedings of the SIGCHI Conference on Human Factors in Computing Systems*, pp. 535–542, 2004.

[MEN 09] MENKOVSKI V., OREDOPE A., LIOTTA A. *et al.*, "Predicting quality of experience in multimedia streaming", *Proceedings of the 7th International Conference on Advances in Mobile Computing and Multimedia*, ACM, pp. 52–59, 2009.

[MEN 10] MENKOVSKI V., EXARCHAKOS G., LIOTTA A., "Machine learning approach for quality of experience aware networks", *2nd International Conference on Intelligent Networking and Collaborative Systems*, pp. 461–466, November 2010.

[MIH 10] MIHOV Y.Y., KASSEV K.M., TSANKOV B.P., "Analysis and performance evaluation of the DRX mechanism for power saving in LTE", *IEEE 26th Convention of Electrical and Electronics Engineers in Israel*, pp. 520–524, November 2010.

[MIL 12] MILLER K., QUACCHIO E., GENNARI G. *et al.*, "Adaptation algorithm for adaptive streaming over HTTP", *19th International Packet Video Workshop*, pp. 173–178, May 2012.

[MOK 11] MOK R., CHAN E., CHANG R., "Measuring the quality of experience of HTTP video streaming", *IFIP/IEEE International Symposium on Integrated Network Management*, pp. 485–492, May 2011.

[MOK 12] MOK R., LUO X., CHAN E. W. W. *et al.*, "QDASH: A QoE-aware DASH System", *Proceedings of the 3rd Multimedia Systems Conference*, pp. 11–22, 2012.

[MUS 12] MUSHTAQ M., SHAHID A., FOWLER S., "QoS-aware LTE downlink scheduler for VoIP with power saving", *IEEE 15th International Conference on Computational Science and Engineering*, December 2012.

[MUS 14a] MUSHTAQ M., AUGUSTIN B., MELLOUK A., "QoE: user profile analysis for multimedia services", *IEEE International Conference on Communications*, pp. 2289–2294, June 2014.

[MUS 14b] MUSHTAQ M., AUGUSTIN B., MELLOUK A., "QoE-based LTE downlink scheduler for VoIP", *IEEE Wireless Communications and Networking Conference*, pp. 2190–2195, April 2014.

[MUS 15] MUSHTAQ M., FOWLER S., MELLOUK A. *et al.*, "QoE/QoS-aware LTE downlink scheduler for VoIP with power saving", *International Journal of Network and Computer Applications*, vol. 51, pp. 29–46, 2015.

[MUS 16] MUSHTAQ M., MELLOUK A., AUGUSTIN B. *et al.*, "QoE Power-Efficient Multimedia Delivery Method for LTE-A", *IEEE Systems Journal*, vol. 10, no. 2, pp. 749–760, 2016.

[NET 15a] NETFLIX, available at: http://www.netflix.com, January 2015.

[NET 15b] NETWORKS M., HD adaptive video streaming, available at: http://www.movenetworkshd.com, January 2015.

[NOR 95] NORROS I., "On the use of fractional Brownian motion in the theory of connectionless networks", *IEEE Journal on Selected Areas in Communications*, vol. 13, no. 6, pp. 953–962, 1995.

[PAL 02] PAL M., MATHER P., "A comparison of decision tree and backpropagation neural network classifiers for land use classification", *IEEE International Geoscience and Remote Sensing Symposium*, vol. 1, pp. 503–505, 2002.

[PAL 10] PALLIS G., "Cloud computing: the new frontier of internet computing", *Internet Computing, IEEE*, vol. 14, no. 5, pp. 70–73, 2010.

[PER 09] PERRUCCI G., FITZEK F.H.P., SASSO G. *et al.*, "On the impact of 2G and 3G network usage for mobile phones' battery life", *European Wireless 2009*, Aalborg, Denmark, May 2009.

[PRA 08] PRANGL M., KOFLER I., HELLWAGNER H., "Towards QoS improvements of TCP-based media delivery", *4th International Conference on Networking and Services*, pp. 188–193, March 2008.

[QUA 13] QUALINET, European network on quality of experience in multimedia systems and services, White Paper, March 2013.

[RAM 09] RAMLI H., BASUKALA R., SANDRASEGARAN K. *et al.*, "Performance of well known packet scheduling algorithms in the downlink 3GPP LTE system", *9th IEEE Malaysia International Conference on Communications*, pp. 815–820, December 2009.

[SEN 06] SENGUPTA S., CHATTERJEE M., GANGULY S. *et al.*, "Improving R-Score of VoIP Streams over WiMax", *IEEE International Conference on Communications*, vol. 2, pp. 866–871, Istanbul, Turkey, 2006.

[SHA 10] SHAIKH J.M., COLLANGE D., "Quality of experience from user and network perspectives", *Springer Journal Annals of Telecommunications*, vol. 65, no. 10, pp. 47–57, 2010.

[SHI 12] SHIRAZIPOUR M., CHARLOT G., LEFEBVRE G. *et al.*, "ConEx based QoE feedback to enhance QoS", *ACM Workshop on Capacity Sharing*, pp. 27–32, December 2012.

[SHY 09] SHYE A., SCHOLBROCK B., MEMIK G., "Into the wild: studying real user activity patterns to guide power optimizations for mobile architectures", *42nd Annual IEEE/ACM International Symposium on Microarchitecture*, pp. 168–178, December 2009.

[SOD 11] SODAGAR I., "The MPEG-DASH Standard for Multimedia Streaming Over the Internet", *MultiMedia, IEEE*, vol. 18, no. 4, pp. 62–67, April 2011.

[TEE 05] TEEVAN J., DUMAIS S.T., HORVITZ E., "Personalizing search via automated analysis of interests and activities", *ACM Proceedings of the 28th Annual International Conference on Research and Development in Information Retrieval*, pp. 449–456, 2005.

[THA 13] THANG T.C., LE H., NGUYEN H. *et al.*, "Adaptive video streaming over HTTP with dynamic resource estimation", *Journal of Communications and Networks*, vol. 15, no. 6, pp. 635–644, 2013.

[TIA 12] TIAN G., LIU Y., "Towards agile and smooth video adaptation in dynamic HTTP streaming", *Proceedings of the 8th International Conference on Emerging Networking Experiments and Technologies*, ACM, USA, New York, pp. 109–120, 2012.

[TRA 14] TRAN H.A., HOCEINI S., MELLOUK A. *et al.*, "QoE-based server selection for content distribution networks", *IEEE Transactions on Computers*, vol. 63, no. 11, pp. 2803–2815, 2014.

[TRU 12] TRUONG T.-H., NGUYEN T.-H., NGUYEN H.-T., "On relationship between quality of experience and quality of service metrics for IMS-based IPTV networks", *IEEE International Conference on Computing and Communication Technologies, Research, Innovation, and Vision for the Future*, pp. 1–6, February 2012.

[UEM 08] UEMURA S., FUKUMOTO N., YAMADA H. *et al.*, "QoS/QoE measurement system implemented on cellular phone for NGN", *5th IEEE Consumer Communications and Networking Conference*, pp. 117–121, January 2008.

[VEN 11] VENKATARAMAN M., CHATTERJEE M., "Inferring video QoE in real time", *IEEE Network*, vol. 25, no. 1, pp. 4–13, 2011.

[WAN 08] WANG B., KUROSE J., SHENOY P. *et al.*, "Multimedia streaming via TCP: an analytic performance study", *ACM Transactions on Multimedia Computing, Communications, and Applications*, vol. 4, no. 2, pp. 16:1–16:22, 2008.

[WU 13] WU J., ZHOU S., NIU Z., "Traffic-aware base station sleeping control and power matching for energy-delay tradeoffs in green cellular networks", *IEEE Transactions on Wireless Communications*, vol. 12, no. 8, pp. 4196–4209, 2013.

[XIA 10] XIAO Y., SAVOLAINEN P., KARPPANEN A. *et al.*, "Practical power modeling of data transmission over 802.11G for wireless applications", *Proceedings of the 1st International Conference on Energy-Efficient Computing and Networking*, ACM, pp. 75–84, 2010.

[YAN 05] YANG S.-R., LIN Y.-B., "Modeling UMTS discontinuous reception mechanism", *IEEE Transactions on Wireless Communications*, vol. 4, no. 1, pp. 312–319, 2005.

[ZHA 04] ZHANG G., JIN W., HU L., "Radar emitter signal recognition based on support vector machines", *Control, Automation, Robotics and Vision Conference*, vol. 2, pp. 826–831, December 2004.

[ZHA 10] ZHANG L., TIWANA B., QIAN Z. *et al.*, "Accurate online power estimation and automatic battery behavior based power model generation for smartphones", *Proceedings of IEEE/ACM/IFIP International Conference on Hardware/Software Codesign and System Synthesis*, pp. 105–114, 2010.

[ZHA 14] ZHAO T., WU J., ZHOU S. *et al.*, "Energy-delay tradeoffs of virtual base stations with a computational-resource-aware energy consumption model", *IEEE International Conference on Communication Systems*, pp. 26–30, November 2014.

[ZHO 08a] ZHOU L., XU H., TIAN H. *et al.*, "Performance analysis of power saving mechanism with adjustable DRX cycles in 3GPP LTE", *IEEE 68th Vehicular Technology Conference*, pp. 1–5, September 2008.

[ZHO 08b] ZHOU X., DREIBHOLZ T., RATHGEB E., "A new server selection strategy for reliable server pooling in widely distributed environments", *Second International Conference on the Digital Society*, pp. 171–177, February 2008.

[ZHO 10] ZHOU R., XIONG Y., XING G. *et al.*, "ZiFi: wireless LAN discovery via ZigBee interference signatures", *Proceedings of the Sixteenth Annual International Conference on Mobile Computing and Networking*, ACM, pp. 49–60, 2010.

[ZHO 12] ZHOU B., WANG J., ZOU Z. *et al.*, "Bandwidth estimation and rate adaptation in HTTP streaming", *International Conference on Computing, Networking and Communications*, pp. 734–738, January 2012.

[ZHO 13a] ZHOU C., LIN C.-W., ZHANG X. *et al.*, "Buffer-based smooth rate adaptation for dynamic HTTP streaming", *Asia-Pacific Signal and Information Processing Association Annual Summit and Conference*, pp. 1–9, October 2013.

[ZHO 13b] ZHOU K., NIKAEIN N., SPYROPOULOS T., "LTE/LTE-A discontinuous reception modeling for machine type communications", *IEEE Wireless Communications Letters*, vol. 2, pp. 102–105, 2013.

[ZIN 10] ZINNER T., HOHLFELD O., ABBOUD O. *et al.*, "Impact of frame rate and resolution on objective QoE metrics", *Second International Workshop on Quality of Multimedia Experience*, June 2010.

Index

Printed in the United States
By Bookmasters